I0428027

STATE SPONSOR OF TERROR: THE GLOBAL THREAT OF IRAN

HEARING

BEFORE THE

SUBCOMMITTEE ON TERRORISM, NONPROLIFERATION, AND TRADE

OF THE

COMMITTEE ON FOREIGN AFFAIRS
HOUSE OF REPRESENTATIVES

ONE HUNDRED FOURTEENTH CONGRESS

FIRST SESSION

FEBRUARY 11, 2015

Serial No. 114–9

Printed for the use of the Committee on Foreign Affairs

Available via the World Wide Web: http://www.foreignaffairs.house.gov/ or
http://www.gpo.gov/fdsys/

U.S. GOVERNMENT PUBLISHING OFFICE

93–283PDF   WASHINGTON : 2015

For sale by the Superintendent of Documents, U.S. Government Publishing Office
Internet: bookstore.gpo.gov   Phone: toll free (866) 512–1800; DC area (202) 512–1800
Fax: (202) 512–2104   Mail: Stop IDCC, Washington, DC 20402–0001

COMMITTEE ON FOREIGN AFFAIRS

EDWARD R. ROYCE, California, *Chairman*

CHRISTOPHER H. SMITH, New Jersey
ILEANA ROS-LEHTINEN, Florida
DANA ROHRABACHER, California
STEVE CHABOT, Ohio
JOE WILSON, South Carolina
MICHAEL T. McCAUL, Texas
TED POE, Texas
MATT SALMON, Arizona
DARRELL E. ISSA, California
TOM MARINO, Pennsylvania
JEFF DUNCAN, South Carolina
MO BROOKS, Alabama
PAUL COOK, California
RANDY K. WEBER SR., Texas
SCOTT PERRY, Pennsylvania
RON DeSANTIS, Florida
MARK MEADOWS, North Carolina
TED S. YOHO, Florida
CURT CLAWSON, Florida
SCOTT DesJARLAIS, Tennessee
REID J. RIBBLE, Wisconsin
DAVID A. TROTT, Michigan
LEE M. ZELDIN, New York
TOM EMMER, Minnesota

ELIOT L. ENGEL, New York
BRAD SHERMAN, California
GREGORY W. MEEKS, New York
ALBIO SIRES, New Jersey
GERALD E. CONNOLLY, Virginia
THEODORE E. DEUTCH, Florida
BRIAN HIGGINS, New York
KAREN BASS, California
WILLIAM KEATING, Massachusetts
DAVID CICILLINE, Rhode Island
ALAN GRAYSON, Florida
AMI BERA, California
ALAN S. LOWENTHAL, California
GRACE MENG, New York
LOIS FRANKEL, Florida
TULSI GABBARD, Hawaii
JOAQUIN CASTRO, Texas
ROBIN L. KELLY, Illinois
BRENDAN F. BOYLE, Pennsylvania

AMY PORTER, *Chief of Staff*   THOMAS SHEEHY, *Staff Director*
JASON STEINBAUM, *Democratic Staff Director*

————

SUBCOMMITTEE ON TERRORISM, NONPROLIFERATION, AND TRADE

TED POE, Texas, *Chairman*

JOE WILSON, South Carolina
DARRELL E. ISSA, California
PAUL COOK, California
SCOTT PERRY, Pennsylvania
REID J. RIBBLE, Wisconsin
LEE M. ZELDIN, New York

WILLIAM KEATING, Massachusetts
BRAD SHERMAN, California
BRIAN HIGGINS, New York
JOAQUIN CASTRO, Texas
ROBIN L. KELLY, Illinois

CONTENTS

STATE SPONSOR OF TERROR: THE GLOBAL THREAT OF IRAN

WEDNESDAY, FEBRUARY 11, 2015

House of Representatives,
Subcommittee on Terrorism, Nonproliferation, and Trade,
Committee on Foreign Affairs,
Washington, DC.

The subcommittee met, pursuant to notice, at 2 o'clock p.m., in room 2172, Rayburn House Office Building, Hon. Ted Poe (chairman of the subcommittee) presiding.

Mr. POE. The subcommittee will come to order.

Without objection, all members may have 5 days to submit statements, objections, questions, and extraneous materials for the record, subject to the length limitation in the rules.

The Iranians are the largest state sponsor of terror in the whole world. Iranian proxy groups like Hezbollah resource and execute attacks around the world. Iranian IRGC and Quds Force troops personally support and engineer attacks on a global scale. These aren't rogue elements; these attacks are directed by the Iranian regime.

This is the very same regime we are in good-faith negotiations with to curb their nuclear ambitions. In my opinion, it is dreaming to believe Iran would uphold any eventual agreement. If sanctions are ultimately lifted through the ongoing negotiations, they should only be sanctions that have to do with Iran's nuclear program. Sanctions put in place for its terrorist activity, although minimal, in my opinion should never be lifted.

Iranian-backed terror plots are a threat to everyone. In 2011, the Iranians plotted to assassinate the Saudi Ambassador to the United States in Washington, DC. That plot, fortunately, was uncovered and stopped before it could be carried out.

Recently, the suspicious death of Argentinian prosecutor Alberto Nisman has raised eyebrows. Nisman was found dead 1 day before he was about to reveal details of Iran's involvement in the 1994 bombing of a Jewish community center in Buenos Aires that killed 85 people—ironic timing, it seems. Given Iran's previous behavior abroad, I believe Nisman's death should be thoroughly investigated to see if the Iranians were involved in that episode.

In Yemen, would-be rebels overthrew the government with the support of—guess who?—the regime in Tehran. Iran has long supported Houthis against Yemen's Sunni tribes. This illegal act also complicates U.S. counterterrorism efforts against AQAP.

(1)

In Iraq, Iran is reenergizing Shia death squads to prop up the government in Baghdad. In fact, these Shia militias that Iran supports, trains, and resources are much more capable than Iraq's own army. There are reports that Iraqi Army units are being led by these Shia militia commanders, controlled by Iran. Even though Malaki is gone, the new Iraqi Prime Minister, al-Abadi, doesn't seem to be trying to distance himself from Iranian control.

And Iranian hands are also in the mischief—they have created mischief all over the attacks and murders of freedom fighters in Camp Liberty and Camp Ashraf. And no one has ever been held accountable for these homicides that have taken place over the last several years against these Iranian dissidents in Iraq.

The lack of inclusive government and Iran's control of the security apparatus does not bode well for the push to defeat ISIL or bring the moderate Sunni tribes into the fold.

In neighboring Syria, Iran is even stronger. Iran virtually controls the Assad regime and helps the murderous dictator cling to power every day. Many believe that if it weren't for Iran, Assad would already have been overthrown.

Iran's power play in the region is paying dividends at the expense of moderate Sunni countries in the region. But Iran's main target is still Israel and Israeli interests around the world. In the last 3 years alone, Iran has killed or tried to kill Israelis, not in Israel but in Bulgaria, India, Thailand, and Georgia, and the list goes on and on. It is truly a worldwide assault on Israel.

Iran must be held accountable for its state sponsorship of acts of terror. It should not be given a pass just because it is talking to us about a different issue, its increased nuclear weapon program. All of these activities are part of Iran's plan to expand its influence and its stature and its terror around the globe.

And now I will recognize the ranking member, Mr. Keating from Massachusetts, for his opening statement.

Mr. KEATING. Thank you, Chairman Poe.

And I would also like to thank our witnesses for being here today.

For over the past 30 years, Iran's stance toward the United States has been antagonistic, to say the least. Despite our renewal of direct talks with Iran, the Iranian regime must understand that, regardless of any progress made on the nuclear issue, the United States and our allies will not turn a blind eye to Iran's established and potentially growing role as a state sponsor of international terrorism.

Working mostly through the Islamic Revolutionary Guard Corps, Quds Force, and its protege, Hezbollah, Iran has continually targeted American citizens and our allies in every corner of the globe. According to the latest State Department country reports on terrorism, Hezbollah, backed by millions of dollars in Iranian funding, has significantly increased its global terrorist activities since 2012. The report states that the United States has seen a resurgence of activity by Iran's Islamic Revolutionary Guard Corps, Quds, the Iranian Ministry of Intelligence and Security, and Tehran's ally Hezbollah.

On January 23, 2013, the Yemeni Coast Guard interdicted an Iranian dhow carrying weapons and explosives likely destined for

Houthi rebels. On February 5, 2013, the Bulgarian Government publicly implicated Hezbollah in July 2012 at the Burgas bombing that killed 5 Israelis and 1 Bulgarian citizen and injured 32 others.

On March 21, 2013, a Cyprus court found that a Hezbollah operative was guilty of charges stemming from his surveillance activities of Israeli tourist targets in 2012. On September 18th, Thailand convicted Atris Hussein, a Hezbollah operative detained by Thai authorities on January 2012.

And on December 30, 2013, a Bahraini Coast Guard interdicted a speedboat attempting to smuggle arms and Iranian explosives, likely destined for armed Shia opposition groups in Bahrain. During an interrogation, the suspects admitted to receiving paramilitary training in Iran.

In addition, we have seen numerous other examples of Iran's direct involvement in or support for terrorist activities, including the 1983 Marine barracks bombing in Lebanon, the 1994 bombing of the AMIA Jewish center in Argentina, the 1996 Khobar Towers bombing in Saudi Arabia, and thwarted terrorist plots in Cyprus, Georgia, Kenya, Thailand, and even right here in Washington, DC, against the Saudi Arabian Ambassador that the chair mentioned.

For the past 3 years, Hezbollah and Quds have funneled money, fighters, and weapons into Syria. Certain senior Quds Force personnel, including General Hassan Shateri, have even died in that struggle.

So, in conclusion, with attention focused on potential diplomatic solutions to the Iranian nuclear crisis, it is important to remind the world that we have not and will not ignore Iran's destabilizing actions around the globe and its continued support to groups who continue to support or plan attacks against American citizens and interests as well as against our allies.

I look to our witnesses today to provide us with more of a complete picture of Iran's activities, what drives its sustained support for international terrorism, and what options the United States has to curtail Iran's support for these groups, particularly through nuclear talks.

With that, I yield back. And thank you, Mr. Chairman.

Mr. POE. I thank the gentleman.

The Chair will now recognize the gentleman from California, Mr. Issa, for an opening statement.

Mr. ISSA. Thank you, Chairman.

Today's hearing is important, but it is not new. We will say a great many things, and very few of them will be new.

Certainly, questions about Armenia's banking relationship with Iran, certainly authorized, pushed, prodded, and cajoled by Russia, is new and concerning when we are looking to Russia, in theory, as an honest broker to help—a destabilizing effect—be thwarted of their nuclear ambitions. But, of course, Russia's involvement makes it very clear that, in fact, all they are really doing is guaranteeing a slow march toward a nuclear Iran.

Sanctions are the subject, Iran is the subject, but we would be remiss if we didn't do two things: Recognize that, all the way back in the early 1980s, the late President Ronald Reagan referred to an evil empire, at that time the Soviet Union. They were evil because of their participation around the world in fomenting the kinds of things that Iran has been fomenting since 1979.

Today, Iran and Russia are partners more than ever before in, in fact, destabilizing activities. As both the chairman and ranking member mentioned, rightfully so, Syria only exists, Hezbollah only exists, Hamas is only a dangerous force because of the direct support from Iran, either directly in money or through its puppet, Syria.

To put it in perspective, today we will talk about Iran as though there is some doubt as to what they might do. But, in fact, I was a 26-year-old Army lieutenant in 1979. I am now a 61-year-old Congressman saying, does it take more than 36 years of direct and constant involvement in terrorism, destabilizing countries around the world, and being involved time and time again in assassinations, kidnaps, and murders?

My point today and, Mr. Chairman, I think what this hearing will show is that Einstein would clearly call it insanity after 36 years of consistently getting the same result from approaches to Iran to believe that this round of negotiations by the administration will yield anything other than what we have had for 36 years since the Ayatollah Khomeini and his gang took over Iran.

And, with that, Mr. Chairman, I want to thank you for the opportunity to make a short opening statement. I look forward to questions, particularly questions on Russia's involvement through Armenia in the backdoor circumvention of the sanctions as they are in place today.

And I yield back.

Mr. POE. The Chair will now recognize another gentleman from California, Mr. Sherman, for his opening statement.

Mr. SHERMAN. Thank you.

There are three forces in the Middle East, or constellation of forces. You have the forces of reason. You have Sunni extremists, typified by Al Qaeda and ISIS. And, finally, and perhaps deserving most of our attention, is the Shiite alliance, quarterbacked by Iran and including Hezbollah, including much of the Baghdad government and certainly the Shiite militias that are run by the Iranians, and, finally, Assad.

We will meet as a full committee in this room tomorrow to discuss ISIS. And everybody is talking about ISIS, and they have videos of evil to show that they are on the cutting edge of unspeakable crimes. But the fact is that the Shiite alliance headed by Iran is far more deadly than ISIS, just in Syria, having killed perhaps as many as 200,000 people, and certainly they have killed more Americans, starting with the Marine barracks in Beirut in—I believe it was 1983.

The Shiite alliance is more dangerous than ISIS. ISIS aspires, may have some capacities as of yet unproven, to carry out directed attacks in the West. As my colleagues in their opening statements have detailed, Iran and its allies have killed people on virtually every continent, save Antarctica.

Now, it is interesting; ISIS, I think, wants to be bombed by the United States. You would have to say they were asking for it, and we have obliged. Assad clearly did not want to be bombed, and the other elements of the Shiite alliance do not want to be bombed by the United States. We have obliged. And before we wage more intense war on ISIS, we have to ask who will fill that space and are we not weakening an enemy of the Shiite alliance without noting that that alliance is a greater threat to us than ISIS.

Finally, though, I would agree that talking to the Iranians is not a bad thing as long as we do not check our skepticism at the door. Ronald Reagan negotiated with the entity he described as an evil empire, and we certainly did business even with Stalin. So talking is fine. You don't make peace with your friends; you make peace with your enemies. But let's not delude ourselves. Iran wants nuclear weapons.

I yield back.

Mr. POE. I thank the gentleman.

The Chair will now recognize the gentleman from Pennsylvania, Mr. Perry, for his opening statement.

Mr. PERRY. Thanks, Mr. Chairman.

Since 1979, Iran has been responsible for countless terrorist plots directly through regime agents or indirectly through proxies like Hamas and Hezbollah. The IRGC is believed to have had a direct role in the 1983 bombing of the U.S. Marine barracks and French military barracks in Beirut, Lebanon, which killed 299 American and French soldiers. After the attacks of September 11, 2001, the Iranian regime assisted the Taliban, Al Qaeda, and radical Shiite militias battling U.S. and allied soldiers in Afghanistan and Iraq. In 2011, the U.S. Government announced it foiled an Iranian terrorist plot to work with Mexican drug cartel members to assassinate the Saudi Ambassador to the United States by bombing a Washington, DC, restaurant he frequented. And, in 2012, the U.S. State Department reported a clear resurgence in Iranian terrorist activities and that Hezbollah's terrorist activities had reached a tempo unseen since the 1990s.

This is nothing new, and it is imperative that we keep these facts, ladies and gentlemen—these facts—in mind during the ongoing nuclear negotiations with the Iranian regime.

And I yield back.

Mr. POE. The gentleman yields back his time.

The Chair will now introduce all four of our witnesses. And we will see how far we can go, because there is a voting process. And after that, we will come back and go from there.

Dr. Fred Kagan is the Christopher DeMuth chair and director of the Critical Threats Project at the American Enterprise Institute. Mr. Kagan is also a former professor of military history at the United States Military Academy at West Point.

Mr. Ilan Berman is vice president of the American Foreign Policy Council. Mr. Berman is widely published on issues of regional security and foreign policy and has also consulted for the CIA, the Department of Defense, and other government agencies.

Mr. Tony Badran is a research fellow at the Foundation for Defense of Democracies. Mr. Badran has written extensively on Hezbollah and focuses his research on countries in the Levant and their regional relationship with militant and terrorist groups.

Dr. Dan Byman is a professor in the Security Studies Program at Georgetown University School of Foreign Service. Dr. Byman is also the research director of the Center for Middle Eastern Policy at the Brookings Institute, where he specializes in Middle East security and counterterrorism.

Dr. Kagan, we will start with you. You have 5 minutes.

STATEMENT OF FREDERICK W. KAGAN, PH.D., CHRISTOPHER DEMUTH CHAIR AND DIRECTOR, CRITICAL THREATS PROJECT, AMERICAN ENTERPRISE INSTITUTE

Mr. KAGAN. Thank you, Mr. Chairman, Ranking Member Keating.

You have stolen a lot of my testimony among the four statements, so I think I will——

Mr. POE. We read your testimony, so we just requoted it.

Mr. KAGAN. And I won't weary your ears by repeating it one more time, but instead I would like to make just a few of the points in here and speak to some of the issues that you have raised in your statements briefly.

We all agree about what the scale of the Iranian threat is, that Iran is acting as an enemy state, that it is engaged in a lot of malign activity in Syria and Iraq and Yemen, and so forth.

I had the opportunity a few weeks ago to spend 4 days in Baghdad at the invitation of Prime Minister Abadi, and it was fascinating. And I would like to share with you, actually, a couple of observations because I think they bear on some of the comments that were made today.

Yes, Quds Force Commander Qasem Soleimani spends a lot of time in Iraq. Yes, Iranian-controlled Shia militias, particularly the Badr Corps, control Diyala province and, I think, largely control the activities of the Fifth Iraqi Army Division in that province. And we certainly have other lethal Shia militias, such as Asaib Ahl al-Haq, which was deployed in Syria and then is now back in Iraq and so on.

But I think that it is too much to say that Abadi is controlled by Iran or desires to be. And I think it is also too much to say that the Iraqi Army is controlled by Iran or desires to be. That was not at all the sense that I got from speaking with numerous Iraqi Army officers and even Shia politicians.

We need to remember that the Iranians are generally as offensive to their neighbors as they are to us, if not more so, and their ability to antagonize is very high. I did absolutely see in the middle of the Green Zone a billboard memorializing Iranian IRGC Brigadier General Taghavi, who was killed around Samarra, which had the IRGC logo at the bottom of it. And that took my breath away because I haven't seen that in Iraq before.

On the other hand, what I generally heard was a desire for the United States to offer an alternative to a very overbearing neighbor that the Iraqis know does not have their best interests at heart, even the Shia.

And I think that, as we reflect on Iraq and we reflect on the role that Iran is playing in Iraq, we need to reflect on our role also, and we need to understand the issue of what alternative we are giving the Iraqis. We are providing a lot. The air campaign is more effective than has been made out, but we could be providing a lot more. And if we would lean into an attempt to help support the new government in Iraq, I think we would have a chance of weaning it away from Iranian control, which is always problematic in an Arab state.

I think one of the things that it is very important to recognize is a threat that emanates from Iran is not just the evil that Tehran intentionally does but the evil that it does unintentionally, as well. It is a pose of the regime that it is an Islamic regime and that it is not a Shia regime. They have not been able to convince hardly anybody except themselves of the truth of that.

And the fact is that the Iranians back sectarian groups pretty much across the board. And those sectarian groups are accelerating and driving sectarian violence throughout the region, which, in turn, is, in my opinion, one of the principal drivers of mobilization for Al Qaeda and its affiliates and radicalization for Muslims in the United States and the West.

So the problem is not simply that we need to get past our hostility with Iran, which I agree is extremely unlikely. The problem is that, even if we decided that we were going to try to ally with Iran in the region and we were going to rely on Iran as a partner, as some have suggested, although no one in this room, they would do it badly, and they would continue to do it badly, and they would continue to cause more problems than they solve, to the extent that they ever solve problems, because Iran is really not much of a problem-solving state. It is much more of a problem-causing state.

I think it is very important to make the point that the nuclear negotiations cannot be separated from concerns about Iranian activities abroad because any relaxation of sanctions, whether they are formally related to terrorist activities or not, will provide a massive influx of resources to the Iranian regime, which it will use in very predictable ways.

It will use those resources, for one thing, as the Supreme Leader has announced and President Rohani has backed, to try to make Iran proof against sanctions anytime in the future. Will they be able to do that? Probably not. Will they be able to weaken our ability to use this economic lever in the future? Almost certainly.

So we need to understand the risk that is inherent in relaxing sanctions in pursuit of a deal that appears to offer modest gains for us at best.

And, lastly, Iran is under tremendous economic pressure from us and from low prices of oil, and that is likely to continue. The military adventurism that they are engaged in is expensive. Supporting the Assad regime is expensive. Doing a variety of other nefarious things that they do are expensive. If we relax sanctions in pursuit of this deal, we will be giving them the resources that they need at a moment of great pinch for them, and you can be certain that a fair percentage of those resources will be diverted to activities that we have articulated here as very problematic.

I am over time, and I don't want to strain your patience. I will just say, if anyone is interested also in talking about the question of how much of a reformer and a moderate President Rohani is, I think that is a topic that bears quite a lot of discussion, as well.

Thank you for the opportunity to speak to you.

Mr. POE. Thank you, Dr. Kagan.

[The prepared statement of Mr. Kagan follows:]

American Enterprise Institute for Public Policy Research

Statement before the House Committee on Foreign Affairs
Subcommittee on Terrorism, Nonproliferation, and Trade on
"State Sponsor of Terror: The Global Threat of Iran"

Beyond Nuclear:
The Increasing Threat from Iran

Frederick W. Kagan

Christopher DeMuth Chair and Director, Critical Threats Project

American Enterprise Institute

February 11, 2015

Frederick W. Kagan
February 11, 2015

Thank you for the opportunity to appear before the committee today. The protracted negotiations about Iran's nuclear program have distracted attention from other aspects of the threat Iran poses to the security of the United States and its allies in the region and around the world. Preventing Iran from acquiring the ability to field a nuclear arsenal is certainly essential, but it is not sufficient, even if any of the deals under discussion were likely to achieve it. Iran has deployed conventional and irregular forces to numerous conflicts throughout the Middle East, and it retains the ability to conduct terrorist operations using its own or proxy forces in Europe, Latin America, and possibly elsewhere. Iran has significantly increased its ballistic missile force over the past few years, both in size and in capability. Tehran also appears to be undertaking an expansion of its conventional military capabilities. The global Iranian threat—independent of the status of its nuclear program—is greater today than it has ever been.

Iranian involvement in the conflicts in Syria and Iraq is well known, but it is worth recalling some of the details. Iran has deployed elements of the Islamic Revolutionary Guards Corps (IRGC) Qods Force, IRGC conventional combat units, advisors from the Law Enforcement Forces, assets of the Ministry of Intelligence and Security, and significant political and economic advisors to help the regime of Bashar al Assad survive. Iran has also encouraged and supported the deployment of thousands of Lebanese Hezbollah conventional forces into Syria as well, a deployment unprecedented in Hezbollah's history.

Iran has deployed a similar mix of forces to Iraq, although on a smaller scale, and without the conventional forces of Hezbollah. The mix includes lethal Iranian-backed Shi'a militias such as Asaib Ahl al Haq, which had been fighting in Syria and was recalled to Iraq after the fall of Fallujah and then Mosul. The commander of the IRGC Qods Force, General Qassem Soleimani, spends a great deal of time in Iraq coordinating the activities of the Shia militias he helped establish years ago and over which he retains control. It is widely reported that Soleimani sleeps in the al Askari Shrine in Samarra, but I also learned on a recent trip to Baghdad that he apparently has a house in the Green Zone as well. Iranian military activities in Iraq are ostentatious. Tehran's proxy militias largely control the province of Diyala and the area around the Samarra Shrine, and they are intertwined with the Iraqi security forces in those areas. The Iraqi Security Forces must tolerate this militia presence because they do not have the wherewithal to replace them. ISF weakness has created an opening that Iranian-backed lethal militias are filling. There was even in mid-late January a large billboard in the center of the Green Zone memorializing an IRGC brigadier general killed in the fighting, with the IRGC logo prominently displayed. By no means all of the Iraqi security forces are under the control of Iran, nor do they wish to be. I heard from political leaders on all sides who have grave concerns about the strength of Iranian proxy militias and the influence Iran is acquiring through its military intervention in Iraq. These forces threaten the sovereignty of the Iraqi state.

Iran has also managed to open up a new front in its regional struggle against Saudi Arabia, by embracing and supporting the al Houthi movement in Yemen. There is a great deal of complexity in the relationship between the Houthis and Iran, but some things are very clear. The leadership of the Houthis has been increasingly vocal in its support for Iran and has praised Iran for backing its movement. The Iranians, for their part, have dramatically increased their rhetorical support for the Houthis, and there are indications that they are providing significant material support as well. The question of Iran's relationship with the Houthis has gained much greater importance following the January Houthi coup d'etat in Sana'a, which has placed that movement firmly in control of Yemeni politics for the moment, although by no means in control of Yemen. Although the Houthis are not in fact orthodox Shia, and Yemen has historically not

Frederick W. Kagan
February 11, 2015

suffered significantly from sectarian conflict, the movement's rise and increasingly close ties with Iran are now inflaming Yemenis along sectarian lines. Al Qaeda in the Arabian Peninsula is thus finding it easier to recruit and operate because it can now position itself as a defender of the Sunni against an Iranian and Shia assault.

The evolution of this tragic dynamic in Yemen epitomizes one of the most serious problems with the idea that the United States could benefit from allying itself with Iran. Iran's leaders have always been at pains to claim that they stand at the head of a nonsectarian Islamic revolution, but they have never been able to persuade the majority of the Muslim community of the truth of that claim. In reality, Iran is seen as a Shia sectarian actor throughout the Arab world, and it preferentially supports Shia proxy groups and individuals. Those groups and individuals tend to be highly sectarian, particularly in light of the rapidly growing sectarian tensions in the region that their activities have helped fuel. Whether Iran's leaders mean to stoke sectarian conflict or not, their actions have been a powerful accelerant to sectarian violence throughout the region, and it appears that they are either unwilling or unable to change. That fact in itself should be enough to dissuade us from the notion that an alliance with Iran, even if one were on offer, would be helpful in solving the region's problems.

There is, however, no such alliance on offer. The Obama administration has repeatedly suggested that the current nuclear negotiations can be part of a larger effort at rapprochement with Iran, much to the consternation of our allies in the region. But the Iranian regime has repeated ad nauseam its unwillingness to engage in any such rapprochement and its refusal to see the negotiations in those terms, despite hints of a possible openness to a sort of temporary détente far removed from any actual reconciliation of interests. Anti-Americanism is a core element of the regime's ideology. It is a critical justification for the regime's concentration of power in its own hands, politically, economically, and socially. The supposed efforts of the United States and the West to undermine the Islamic Republic by exporting our culture and ideas to Iran's people form a significant excuse the government uses to sustain one of the most sophisticated and draconian censorship regimes on the planet. Any serious rapprochement with the United States would badly undermine the regime's justifications for this and many other oppressive activities it regards as essential to its survival, and it is almost impossible to imagine the current leadership embracing any such approach.

We must assume, therefore, that Tehran will continue to see the United States as a dangerous and aggressive enemy regardless of the outcome of the nuclear negotiations. Iran's leaders will continue to believe that America is attempting to build an alliance of Arab states and Israel with the aim of containing Iran and eventually bringing down the current regime. Iran has held this view without alteration since the 1979 Revolution, and nothing that President Obama can do in the next two years is likely to change it. Iran will therefore continue to be an enemy state, preparing itself for either offensive or defensive war against the United States and its allies in the region, with or without a nuclear program.

The further relaxation of sanctions on Iran as a consequence of any nuclear deal will dramatically assist Iran in these preparations. Iran's leaders have articulated in great detail how they would use additional post-sanctions funding to address major structural problems in their economy. The Supreme Leader and President Rouhani have described an economic doctrine they call "Resistance Economy," which aims to ensure that Iran will never be vulnerable to sanctions again in the future.[1] An influx of money and investment at this stage will also fuel Iran's ability to sustain the military and paramilitary forces it has deployed around the region and to fund its violent and sectarian proxies. A nuclear deal without some sort of real rapprochement, therefore, will actually increase the Iranian military threat to America's interests and allies in the Middle East and possibly beyond.

It would certainly be desirable to make a verifiable deal with Iran that insured that the Islamic Republic would not be able to develop and field a nuclear arsenal. Judging from the leaks coming from negotiating teams on both sides, however, it does not appear that any such deal is on the table. We must recognize in any case the stakes involved in gambling on a partial deal, and the price we are likely to pay in increasing regional and even global threats from Iran as sanctions are lifted. One thing is absolutely certain, however. A deal with Iran that addresses only narrow technical issues related to the nuclear program does not even begin to address the challenge Iran poses to the United States, its allies, and the West. Addressing that challenge would require developing a coherent and nuanced strategy toward Iran, something that is notably absent today.

---

[1] Amir Toumaj, "Iran's Economy of Resistance: Implications for Future Sanctions," AEI's Critical Threats Project, November 17, 2014, http://www.irantracker.org/analysis/toumaj-irans-resistance-economy-implications-for-sanctions-november-17-2014.

Mr. POE. Mr. Berman, 5 minutes.

STATEMENT OF MR. ILAN I. BERMAN, VICE PRESIDENT, AMERICAN FOREIGN POLICY COUNCIL

Mr. BERMAN. Thank you, sir.

Chairman Poe, Ranking Member Keating, thank you very much for the opportunity to appear before you today to discuss the global threat, the truly global threat, of Iran.

This is a subject that unfortunately has not been addressed seriously or comprehensively over the last year and a half. Instead, if I could borrow a phrase from the late New York Senator Daniel Patrick Moynihan, we have defined Iran's deviancy down. We have concerned ourselves with the prospects of achieving a deal over Iran's nuclear program to the exclusion of a serious conversation about other aspects of Iran's rogue behavior. And we have neglected to think deeply and to focus on what Iran actually says and what it believes.

That is a very good place to start, I think. The roots of Iran's current confrontational world view stretch back to the Islamic Revolution that occurred 36 years ago this month. That event enshrined the idea of exporting the revolution as a cardinal regime principle for Iran's new government, and it is an idea that remains very much in effect today.

The State Department's most recent report on global terrorism trends, which all of you gentlemen referenced, makes a point of demonstrating that, even though Iran is constrained by international pressure, Iranian rogue activity globally is on the rise. Iran, in other words, is on the march.

It is doing so in multiple theaters, from Syria to the Palestinian territories, to Africa, to even Eurasia. Because my time is limited here, let me focus simply on two.

The first is Latin America, which is very much in the headlines today because of the suspected murder of Argentine prosecutor Alberto Nisman. But Iran's intrusion into the region is not a new phenomenon.It dates back to the early 1980s, when Iran helped Lebanon's Hezbollah set up shop in the tri-border region where Brazil, Argentina, and Paraguay intersect. That beachhead, in turn, allowed Hezbollah to carry out the 1992 attack on the Israeli Embassy in Buenos Aires and, 2 years later, to carry out the attack on the AMIA center, which ranks as the largest incident of Islamist terrorism to date in the Western Hemisphere other than 9/11.

But, over the past decade, Iran's regional footprint has gotten much larger. Beginning in 2005, Iran systematically expanded its contacts throughout the region, leveraging the radical regime of Hugo Chavez in Venezuela as a gateway to expand its ties to what are called the Bolivarian nations, the radical, leftist, anti-American nations of the region, in particular to the regime of Evo Morales in Bolivia and of Rafael Correa in Ecuador.

But these formal ties have been mirrored by a large and effective clandestine network that Iran has succeeded in erecting in the region. Mr. Nisman, in his May 2013 report, detailed that Iran had succeeded over the preceding 30 years in establishing a terror network encompassing no fewer than 8 countries in the region.

Via that network, Iran has been able to attempt at least three attacks on the U.S. homeland over the past decade: The 2007 attempt to blow up fuel tanks underneath JFK Airport in New York; the fall 2011 plan for widespread cyber attacks, to be carried out jointly by Venezuela and Iran; and, most famously, the foiled attempt to assassinate Saudi Envoy Adel al-Jubeir in a Washington restaurant in October 2011.

In short, Iran's presence in the Americas is growing, and so is the threat that it has the potential to pose to the U.S. homeland from the Western Hemisphere.

The second but equally germane field where Iran is expanding it activities is cyberspace. This capability, which has manifested since the popularization of Stuxnet in 2009 and 2010, is not simply defensive in nature. It is aimed at both limiting access to the Internet among ordinary Iranians, a campaign domestically, and also an external campaign aimed at targeting Western institutions and infrastructure.

The cybersecurity firm Cylance, in a December 2014 report, noted that, since 2012, Iranian hackers have attacked government agencies and companies in countries such as Saudi Arabia, South Korea, Turkey, and beyond. Here in the United States, Iranian entities have targeted financial institutions like Bank of America and JPMorgan Chase and have also hacked the Navy's unclassified email network. The study cites Israeli expert Gabi Siboni as saying that Iran should be considered a first-tier cyber power. It is one that can cause considerable harm to the United States via cyberspace if it chooses to do so.

Sadly, a sober assessment of Iran's threat potential and its growing activism has been obscured by the ongoing talks over Iran's nuclear program. Today, we have become incentivized not to call attention to Iranian activities or to Iranian ideology lest a tactical bargain with the regime over its nukes becomes more difficult to obtain as a result. But, as I hope I have pointed out, making that choice, making that bargain, is something that we do at our great peril and to our great detriment.

Thank you.

Mr. POE. Thank you very much.

[The prepared statement of Mr. Berman follows:]

State Sponsor of Terror: The Global Threat of Iran

Statement before the
U.S. House of Representatives Committee on Foreign Affairs
Subcommittee on Terrorism, Nonproliferation, and Trade

Ilan Berman
Vice President
American Foreign Policy Council

February 11, 2015

Chairman Poe, distinguished members of the Subcommittee:

It is an honor to appear before you today to discuss the global threat posed by the Islamic Republic of Iran. It is an issue that has received far too little attention over the past year-and-a-half.

Since the start of negotiations between Iran and the P5+1 powers in November of 2013, the attention of the United States and its diplomatic partners has focused almost exclusively on one aspect of Iran's activities, its nuclear program. For the Obama administration, reaching some sort of durable compromise with the Iranian regime over its nuclear ambitions has become an overriding objective. As Deputy National Security Advisor Ben Rhodes told a meeting of political activists in January of 2014, securing such a deal is considered by the White House to be as significant as its previous success on healthcare, the signature initiative of President Obama's first term.[1]

Moreover, with the rise of the Islamic State terrorist group in Iraq, the White House has gravitated toward the notion that Iran also can serve as a constructive security partner. Administration officials have said that they see a role for Iran in the international coalition that Washington is now erecting,[2] and tactical coordination between Tehran and Washington on combat operations is widely understood to be taking place.

In its outreach, the Administration has been driven in no small measure by the belief that current contacts can be successfully parlayed into something substantially bigger: a true reconciliation between Washington and Tehran. This belief has led officials in Washington to systematically downplay instances of Iranian rogue behavior, chief among them the Iranian regime's fomentation of international terrorism.

A REGIME IMPERATIVE

Iran's intimate relationship with terrorism is a function of the ideological worldview that continues to animate the present regime in Tehran.

That outlook can be traced back to the 1960s and 1970s, when the Islamic Republic's founder, the Ayatollah Ruhollah Khomeini, languished in exile, first in Iraq and then in France. During that time, Khomeini became convinced of the need for Shi'ite empowerment and global Islamic revolution. As a result, the overthrow of Shah Mohammad Reza Pahlavi in 1979 was not seen simply as a domestic regime change. Rather, It was also viewed by Khomeini and his followers as the start of a political process that would usher in the dominance of Islam "in all the countries of the world."[3]

Accordingly, the preamble of the country's 1979 constitution proclaimed that the Islamic Republic's armed forces "will be responsible not only for safeguarding the borders, but also for accomplishing an ideological mission, that is, the Jihad for the sake of God, as well as for struggling to open the way for the sovereignty of the Word of God throughout the world."[4] Iran's revolution, in other words, was intended from the start to be an export commodity.

The first formative years of Khomeini's regime therefore saw his government erect an elaborate domestic infrastructure for the support and propagation of terrorism abroad—an effort that spanned multiple ministries and agencies, and included the investment of hundreds of millions of dollars in the cause of Islamic "resistance" globally.[5] The Islamic Republic also became a haven and source of support for third world radicals, from Palestinian resistance fighters to Latin American leftist revolutionaries.[6]

The death of Khomeini in the late 1980s—and a period of sustained economic and political stagnation in the 1990s—led many in the West to believe that Iran had entered a "post-revolutionary" era. That hope, however, turned out to be fleeting. During the 1990s, Iran's regime continued to work diligently to improve its global position and "export" its uncompromising version of political Islam—albeit more subtly and judiciously than it had the preceding decade. And over the past dozen years, Iran's revolutionary fervor has returned with a vengeance.

Today, very much in line with Khomeini's famous 1980 dictum that his regime must "strive to export our revolution throughout the world,"[7] the Islamic Republic is pursuing a global insurgent agenda, acting either directly (via its feared clerical army, the Islamic Revolutionary Guard Corps [IRGC]) or through a broad range of proxy groups and aligned non-state actors, from Lebanon's Hezbollah to the Palestinian Hamas movement to Shi'ite militias in Iraq.

GLOBAL REACH

While the full scope of Iran's activities is far broader than could be comfortably covered here, several areas of its current activity deserve particular attention.

Syria
Since the start of the civil war there in March of 2011, Iran has waged what amounts to a proxy war in Syria. While publicly it has sought to portray a constructive image vis-à-vis the crisis, the Iranian regime has quietly pursued a much more assertive—and destructive—role. Iran, for example, has deployed a large IRGC contingent to the Syrian battlefield, including hundreds of trained snipers who have helped to reinforce Syrian forces and increase their lethality against Syria's opposition.[8] Together with its Lebanese proxy Hezbollah, it has also played a key role in organizing pro-Assad militias among the country's Alawite and Shi'a communities, as well as coordinating pro-regime foreign fighters from Iraq, Yemen, Lebanon and—most recently—Afghanistan. [9] Iranian officials have boasted that these "popular committees" now total upward of 50,000 fighters in number, and benefit from training provided to them both in Iran and in Lebanon.[10]

Iran's objectives in this effort are two-fold. Most immediately, Iran's aid is intended to shore up the stability of the Assad regime, its most important regional partner. More broadly, however, Iran sees its involvement in Syria as a direct blow against the "Great Satan," the United States. "Since Syria was and continues to be part of the Islamic resistance front and the Islamic Revolution, it provokes the anger of the Americans," IRGC commander Mohammad Ali Jafari explained on Iranian television in April of 2014.[11] Alaeddin Boroujerdi, the Chairman of the Iranian Parliament's National Security and Foreign Policy Committee, put it even more bluntly. "We have won in Syria," he told reporters in May of 2014. "The regime will stay. The Americans have lost it."[12]

Palestinian Territories
In the summer of 2014, a new round of hostilities broke out between Israel and the Hamas terrorist movement in the Gaza Strip. Israeli officials termed the outcome of the fifty-day conflict to be a "strategic tie."[13] Yet the benefits were undeniably greater for Hamas, which used the war as a bid for continued relevance—and as a way to reestablish strategic ties with Iran, which had been virtually severed over the preceding three years as a result of conflicting approaches to Syria. As a result, the strategic partnership between Iran and Hamas is now back on track—and the likelihood of a future conflict between Israel and an unrepentant, strengthened Hamas is high.

Iran's stake in the Palestinian Territories is far larger than simply Hamas, however. Since the 1990s, the Islamic Republic has played a leading role in the West

Bank and Gaza Strip through its political support of Palestinian violence, its funding for an array of Palestinian "rejectionist" groups, and its provision of weapons to disparate Palestinian factions. That assistance continues; earlier this month, a top commander in Iran's Islamic Revolutionary Guard Corps (IRGC) called for his government to increase its presence and activities in the West Bank and Gaza Strip as a way of holding Israel at risk, and preventing the possibility of unilateral Israeli military action against Iran's nuclear program.[14]

Iraq

Over the past year, the rise of the Islamic State terrorist group has captured global attention, and nudged Tehran and Washington into tacit alignment. This has served to obscure the fact that, over the past decade, the Islamic Republic has pursued a complex multi-pronged strategy on the territory of its western neighbor. That effort has involved, *inter alia*, the cooptation of various Iraqi politicians; political and material support to both Sunni and Shi'ite militias; the massive infiltration of Iranian paramilitary forces and proxies onto Iraqi soil, and; the provision of a wide spectrum of lethal weaponry (including improvised explosive devices) to Iraqi insurgents fighting the Coalition.[15] The human toll of this effort has been immense. In August of 2010, then-U.S. Ambassador to Iraq James Jeffrey estimated that fully a quarter of U.S. casualties in Iraq since the start of Operation Iraqi Freedom in 2003 were attributable to Iranian-linked groups operating against the Coalition.[16]

Iran's geopolitical goals were clear. "Iran has a robust program to exert influence in Iraq in order to limit American power-projection capability in the Middle East, ensure the Iraqi government does not pose a threat to Iran, and build a reliable platform for projecting influence further abroad," a 2008 study by the Combatting Terrorism Center at West Point explained.[17] And today, Iran is closer to this objective than ever before. With Iraq's government in continuing disarray despite an October 2014 parliamentary election and a change of political leadership, and amid signals from Washington that sustained U.S. boots on the ground are simply out of the question in the fight against the Islamic State, Iran has emerged as what is perhaps the best long-term guarantor of Iraq's security.

Afghanistan

Over the past decade, Iran has worked diligently to expand its influence on the territory of its eastern neighbor. It has done so by coopting and subverting the independence of the post-Taliban government of Hamid Karzai through political pressure and economic bribes, and by simultaneously forging an alternative center of gravity in Afghanistan's western provinces. It also has sought to deny influence to others, most prominently the United States and its allies. In its 2012 *Country Reports on Terrorism*, the State Department noted that, "[s]ince 2006, Iran has arranged arms shipments to select Taliban members, including small arms and associated ammunition, rocket propelled grenades, mortar rounds, 107mm rockets, and plastic explosives." According to the same assessment, "Iran has shipped a large number of weapons to Kandahar, Afghanistan, aiming to increase its influence in this key province." It also "trained Taliban elements on small unit tactics, small arms, explosives, and indirect fire weapons, such as mortars, artillery, and rockets."[18]

Iran's assistance has significantly expanded the lethality of these forces, at considerable human cost to the United States and its Coalition allies.

Latin America

In October of 2011, U.S. officials went public with details of a foiled Iranian plot to assassinate Saudi Arabia's ambassador to the United States at a DC restaurant. Attorney General Eric Holder noted at the time that the plot was "directed and approved by elements of the Iranian government and, specifically, senior members of the Quds Force," the IRGC's elite paramilitary unit.[19] The thwarted plot was far from unique, however; Iran has targeted the U.S. homeland on at least two other occasions over the past decade. The first was an unsuccessful 2007 plot by a Guyanese national linked to Iran to blow up fuel tanks underneath New York's John F. Kennedy Airport.[20] The second was a plan by Venezuelan and Iranian diplomats to use Mexican hackers to penetrate U.S. defense and intelligence facilities and launch widespread cyber attacks in the United States.[21]

These attempts were made possible by an expanding Iranian strategic footprint in the Americas. In its 2010 report to Congress on Iran's military power, the Pentagon noted that the Qods Force has become deeply involved in the Americas, stationing "operatives in foreign embassies, charities and religious/cultural institutions to foster relationships with people, often building on existing socio-economic ties with the well-established Shia Diaspora," and even carrying out "paramilitary operations to support extremists and destabilize unfriendly regimes."[22] These activities, however, are just the tip of the iceberg. In his May 2013 indictment, Argentine prosecutor Alberto Nisman detailed that over the past three decades, Iran has succeeded in quietly erecting a network of intelligence bases and covert centers in no fewer than eight Latin American countries: Brazil, Paraguay, Uruguay, Chile, Colombia, Guyana, Trinidad and Tobago, and Suriname.[23] This infrastructure was instrumental in allowing Iranian proxies to carry out the 1994 AMIA bombing, as well as to plot subsequent attacks, and remains both intact and functioning. (Not coincidentally, Iran is being eyed as a culprit in Nisman's suspected murder last month, which took place on the eve of his testimony before the Argentine Congress regarding his government's collusion with Tehran.)

Africa

In May of 2013, Nigerian security forces raided a house on the outskirts of Bompai, in the country's northern Kano State. They found a massive military stash, including anti-tank weapons, rocket propelled guns and landmines.[24] Three men were subsequently arrested in connection to the raid, all of them Lebanese-Nigerian nationals. In subsequent interrogations, the suspects confessed to having received training from Hezbollah, and one of them detailed that he had gotten orders from a top Hezbollah commander to surveil several targets in the Nigerian capital, including the Israeli embassy there, and to obtain an aerial photo of the city for targeting purposes.[25]

To be sure, Hezbollah has had an African presence for the better part of a quarter century. Beginning in the late 1980s, the group, operating through the continent's numerous and well-established Shi'a communities, transformed Africa into a major base for fundraising, becoming involved in the continent's notorious "blood diamond" trade and establishing a number of front companies to funnel money from Africa back to the Middle East.[26] The region likewise became a notable recruiting base for the group, which—working in tandem with the IRGC—has made concerted efforts to enlist disaffected African Shi'a in "resistance" against Israel and the West.[27] In recent years, however, the scope and pace of these activities have expanded. "Iran has stepped up its attempts to build a sphere of influence in Africa," according to Israeli counterterrorism expert Ely Karmon, and is working "to develop bases within certain states in Africa for wider terrorist and subversion activities throughout the continent, focusing on Israeli and Jewish targets."[28] These bases extend beyond Nigeria to a number of other regional states, including Kenya, Sierra Leone, Senegal, Cote d'Ivoire, and Senegal.

Europe
In July of 2012, a pre-positioned bomb detonated on a passenger bus full of Israeli tourists in the Bulgarian Black Sea resort town of Burgas, killing six people and injuring thirty-two others. In the days after the attack, Israeli Prime Minister Benjamin Netanyahu linked the bombing to Hezbollah and its chief sponsor, Iran, terming it to be part of a "global Iranian terror onslaught" targeting his country's interests and citizens worldwide.[29] That verdict was confirmed seven months later, when the Bulgarian government published its official findings, which identified the two suspects in the bombing as operatives of the Lebanese militia.[30]

Like its activities in Africa, Hezbollah's presence in Europe is not a new phenomenon. The organization has been active on the continent since the early 1980s, and engaged in a spate of terrorist activity there during that time (including a plane hijacking in 1984, bombings in Spain, Denmark and France the following year, and a rash of bombings in Paris between 1985 and 1986). Over time, however, the militia shifted its focus back to the Middle East, and Europe—once a target— became seen as primarily a base, and a "launching pad" for operations elsewhere.[31] Of late, however, the growing global activism of Hezbollah's enabler, Iran, has increasingly transformed Europe from a base of operations for Iran's chief terrorist proxy back into a target of it. The August 2012 Burgas bombing was a reflection of this trend, which now poses a real danger to European security.

Cyberspace
Over the past several years, Iran has manifested a growing, and increasingly aggressive, presence in cyberspace. This effort can be traced back, at least in part, to the targeting of Iran's nuclear program by the Stuxnet cyberworm in 2009/2010 and other subsequent intrusions—attacks which convinced Iran's leadership that they were engaged in a conflict with the West in cyberspace. But Iran's cyber activities are not simply defensive in nature; over the past three years, Iranian and Iranian-linked entities have carried out attacks on a number of high-value targets abroad, among them U.S. financial institutions (Bank of America, JPMorgan Chase and Citigroup), foreign energy firms (Saudi AramCo) and several defense contractors.

The scope of Iran's offensive was outlined in detail in December of 2014 by San Diego-based cybersecurity firm Cylance.[32] "Since at least 2012, Iranian actors have directly attacked, established persistence in, and extracted highly sensitive materials from the networks of government agencies and major critical infrastructure companies in the following countries: Canada, China, England, France, Germany, India, Israel, Kuwait, Mexico, Pakistan, Qatar, Saudi Arabia, South Korea, Turkey, United Arab Emirates, and the United States," the study notes. Targets of Iranian cyber attack identified by Cylance include oil and gas firms in Kuwait, Turkey, Qatar and France, aviation hubs in South Korea and Pakistan, energy and utilities companies in Canada and the U.S., and government agencies in the U.S., UAE and Qatar. This, however, may represent merely the tip of the iceberg. "As Iran's cyber warfare capabilities continue to morph... the probability of an attack that could impact the physical world at a national or global level is rapidly increasing," the report concludes.

DEFINING IRAN'S DEVIANCY DOWN

In the 1990s, New York Senator Daniel Patrick Moynihan popularized the term "defining deviancy down" in warning about the dangers of an increasingly lax American criminal justice system. Today, that same admonition could be applied to U.S. policy toward Iran.

In its pursuit of a nuclear deal, the Obama administration has turned a blind eye to the Iranian regime's ideological direction, and to its destructive behavior abroad. Worse still, the White House has become incentivized not to pay any heed to, or call attention to, what the Iranian regime truly thinks, says and does, lest it prejudice prospects for political alignment between Washington and Tehran.

This represents a critical error. Iran's rogue behavior spans a broad spectrum of subversive activities in virtually every corner of the world. Furthermore, the Iranian leadership remains revolutionary in outlook and insurgent in its behavior.

It also increasingly convinced that it is winning. That was the message of Supreme Leader Ali Khamenei's September 2014 speech to Iran's Assembly of Experts, the regime's premier religious supervisory body. The existing international system "was in the process of change," Khamenei asserted, and a "new order is being formed." These changes, he made clear, are a mortal blow to the West, and a boon to Iran: "The power of the West on their two foundations—values and thoughts and the political and military—have become shaky."[33]

The message is unmistakable. The Islamic Republic sees an increasingly favorable international environment, and is stepping up its activism in response. Responding to it will be one of the most significant challenges facing the United States in the years ahead.

[1] As cited in Matthew Continetti, "The Coming Détente with Iran," *Washington Free Beacon*, October 31, 2014, http://freebeacon.com/columns/the-coming-detente-with-iran/.

[2] Jesse Byrnes, "Secy. Kerry Says Iran can Help Defeat ISIS," *The Hill*, September 19, 2014, http://thehill.com/blogs/blog-briefing-room/news/218391-iran-can-help-defeat-isis-kerry-says.

[3] Ruhollah Khomeini, as quoted in Robin Wright, *Sacred Rage: The Wrath of Militant Islam* (New York: Simon & Schuster, 1986), 21.

[4] Preamble, *Constitution of the Islamic Republic of Iran*, October 24, 1979, http://www.oefre.unibe.ch/law/icl/ir00000_.html.

[5] For a detailed overview of Iran's terror infrastructure, see Ilan Berman, *Tehran Rising: Iran's Challenge to the United States* (Lanham, MD: Rowman & Littlefield, 2005), 3-30.

[6] Robin Wright, *Sacred Rage: The Wrath of Militant Islam* (New York: Simon & Schuster, 1986), 21, 32-35.

[7] As cited in Hamid Algar, *Islam and Revolution Writings and Declarations of Imam Khomeini (1941-1980)* (North Haledon, NJ: Mizan Press, 1981), 286-287.

[8] Luke McKenna, "Syria is Importing Iranian Snipers to Murder Anti-Government Protesters," *Business Insider*, January 27, 2012, http://www.businessinsider.com/syria-is-importing-iranian-snipers-to-murder-anti-government-protesters-2012-1.

[9] See, for example, Farnaz Fassihi, "Iran Recruiting Afghan Refugees to Fight for Regime in Syria," *Wall Street Journal*, May 15, 2014, http://online.wsj.com/news/articles/SB10001424052702304908304579564161508613846?mg=reno64-wsj&url=http%3A%2F%2Fonline.wsj.com%2Farticle%2FSB10001424052702304908304579564161508613846.html.

[10] Babak Dehghanpisheh, "Elite Iranian Unit's Commander Says His Forces are in Syria," *Washington Post*, September 16, 2012, http://www.washingtonpost.com/world/middle_east/elite-iranian-units-commander-says-his-forces-are-in-syria/2012/09/16/431ff096-0028-11e2-b257-e1c2b3548a4a_story.html; Karen DeYoung and Joby Warrick, "Iran, Hezbollah Build Militia Networks in Syria in Event that Assad Falls, Officials Say," *Washington Post*, February 10, 2013, http://www.washingtonpost.com/world/national-security/iran-hezbollah-build-militia-networks-in-syria-in-event-that-assad-falls-officials-say/2013/02/10/257a41c8-720a-11e2-ac36-3d8d9dcaa2e2_story.html?hpid=z2.

[11] "Iranian Revolutionary Guard Corps Commander Jafari: We Support Resistance to U.S. and Israel in Syria and Elsewhere in the Region," Middle East Media Research Institute *Clip* no. 4272, April 21, 2014, http://www.memritv.org/clip/en/4272.htm.

[12] Simon Tisdall, "Iran and Assad have Won in Syria, Say Top Tehran Foreign Policy Figures," *Guardian* (London), May 12, 2014, http://www.theguardian.com/world/2014/may/11/syria-crisis-iran-assad-won-war-tehran.

[13] Author's interviews with Israeli officials, Jerusalem and Tel Aviv, Israel, September 2014.

[14] "Iran Revolutionary Guards General Calls for Greater Foothold in West Bank and Gaza," *Algemeiner*, February 2, 2015, http://www.algemeiner.com/2015/02/02/iran-revolutionary-guards-general-calls-for-greater-foothold-in-west-bank-and-gaza/.

[15] Kimberly Kagan, "Iran's Proxy War Against the United States and the Iraqi Government," Institute for the Study of War *Iraq Report*, May 2006-August 20, 2007, https://www.understandingwar.org/sites/default/files/reports/IraqReport06.pdf.

[16] "Quarter of US Iraq Deaths Due to Iran Groups – Envoy," Reuters, August 26, 2010, http://www.reuters.com/article/2010/08/26/idUSLDE67P22D.

[17] Joseph Felter and Brian Fishman, "Iranian Strategy in Iraq: Politics and 'Other Means,'" Combatting Center at West Point *Occasional Paper*, October 13, 2008, http://reap2-ws1.stanford.edu/publications/iranian_strategy_in_iraq_politics_and_other_means/.

[18] U.S. Department of State, Office of the Coordinator for Counterterrorism, "Chapter 3. State Sponsors of Terrorism Overview," in *Country Reports on Terrorism 2012*, May 2013, http://www.state.gov/j/ct/rls/crt/2012/209985.htm.

[19] Charles Savage and Scott Shane, "Iranians Accused of a Plot to Kill Saudis' U.S. Envoy," *New York Times*, October 11, 2011, http://www.nytimes.com/2011/10/12/us/us-accuses-iranians-of-plotting-to-kill-saudi-envoy.html?pagewanted=all.

[20] "'Iran Set Up Terrorist Network in Latin America,'" Reuters, May 30, 2013, http://www.jpost.com/Iranian-Threat/News/Prosecutor-Iran-set-up-terrorist-networks-in-Latin-America-314793.

[21] "La Amenaza Irani," *Univision*, December 9, 2011, http://noticias.univision.com/article/786870/2011-12-09/documentales/la-amenaza-irani/la-amenaza-irani.

[22] Department of Defense, *Unclassified Report on Military Power of Iran*, April 2010, http://www.armscontrolwonk.com/file_download/226/2010_04_19_Unclass_Report_on_Iran_Military.pdf.

[23] Guido Nejmakis, "Iran Set Up Terrorist Networks in Latin America: Argentine Prosecutor," Reuters, May 29, 2013, http://www.reuters.com/article/2013/05/29/us-argentina-iran-idUSBRE94S1F420130529.

[24] "JTF Uncovers Lebanese Terror Cell in Kano... Mustapha Fawaz, Co-Owner of Popular Amigo Supermarket Arrested," *Xclusive Nigeria*, May 31, 2013, http://www.exclusivenigeria.com/index.php/politics/item/698-jtf-uncovers-lebanese-terror-cell-in-kanomustapha-fawaz-co-owner-of-popular-amigo-supermarket-arrested.

[25] Ibid; Ikechukwu Nnochiri, "Hezbolla: I got Order to Survey Israeli Embassy in Nigeria – FAWAZ," *Vanguard* (Abuja), August 1, 2013, http://www.vanguardngr.com/2013/08/hezbolla-i-got-order-to-survey-israeli-embassy-in-nigeria-fawaz/.

[26] Matthew Levitt, *Hezbollah: The Global Footprint of Lebanon's Party of God* (Washington, DC: Georgetown University Press, 2013), 261.

[27] Ibid., 265.

[28] Ely Karmon, "Out of Iran, into Africa: Hezbollah's Scramble for Africa," *Ha'aretz* (Tel Aviv), June 17, 2013, http://www.haaretz.com/news/features/.premium-1.530327.

[29] "Israel Blames Iran in Deadly Bulgaria Bus Blast," Associated Press, July 18, 2012, http://www.cbsnews.com/news/israel-blames-iran-in-deadly-bulgaria-bus-blast/.

[30] "Bulgaria Says Hezbollah Behind Burgas Bombing," Reuters, February 5, 2013, http://www.reuters.com/article/2013/02/05/us-bulgaria-bombing-idUSBRE91400020130205.

[31] Matthew Levitt, testimony before the House International Relations Committee Subcommittee on Europe and Emerging Threats, April 27, 2005, http://wwwa.house.gov/international_relations/109/lev042705.pdf.

[32] Cylance, *Operation Cleaver*, December 2, 2014, http://www.cylance.com/assets/Cleaver/Cylance_Operation_Cleaver_Report.pdf.

[33] See Arash Karami, "Ayatollah Khamenei Urges Iran to Prepare for 'New World Order,'" *Al-Monitor*, September 5, 2014, http://www.al-monitor.com/pulse/originals/2014/09/khamenei-new-world-order.html#.

Mr. POE. Mr. Badran, you can have 5 minutes, and then we will get Dr. Byman. And then we will break for votes and then come back for questions, so everyone knows the order of events. Thank you very much.

Mr. Badran, you can proceed.

STATEMENT OF MR. TONY BADRAN, RESEARCH FELLOW, FOUNDATION FOR DEFENSE OF DEMOCRACIES

Mr. BADRAN. Thank you, Chairman Poe and Ranking Member Keating. Thank you very much for inviting me to this very timely hearing.

And I will talk a little bit about the organic relationship between Iran and Hezbollah but also the template that they have put together in the Middle East and how this poses a threat to U.S. interests there. I will give a brief synopsis, and I will be glad to talk about the details with answering your questions.

The nature of the Iranian threat extends beyond terrorism. A senior Iranian official put it recently to Reuters, and he says, everything is about the balance of power in the region. So they are focused on that issue.

And sensing that their moment has arrived, the Iranians are in the middle of an aggressive region-wide expansionist drive. They openly brag today about controlling four Arab capitals—Baghdad, Beirut, Damascus, and Sana'a. In each of these capitals, the Iranians have developed proxies either by creating new militias on the Hezbollah model or by coopting local actors. And they are uses these proxies to extend Iran's reach and integrating them into a broader strategy targeting U.S. allies and interests.

And Hezbollah is at the center of this strategy. Since the very beginning of the Islamic revolutionary regime, that was when Hezbollah was created, and its progenitors sought to spawn movements along that model in the Arab world to allow them to embed themselves in Arab societies and project influence.

As Representative Issa said, this is not new. They are the same faces. The Defense Minister of Iran is the same person who was the IRGC commander in Lebanon at the time of the barracks bombing in Beirut. What is new, what the Iranians hadn't counted on, however, is that the United States would one day acquiesce to this bid of regional hegemony.

When Iranian officials talk about the various assets that they are supporting in the Arab world, they have a point of reference, which is the Hezbollah model. It is a specific template which consists of developing political-military structures parallel to central Arab governments, especially where those governments are weak. And much like the Soviet Union before, they set up proxies to dominate states.

So first there is what is called the Basij model, in reference to the Iranian paramilitary group. This is what we are seeing the Iranians now do in Iraq with the so-called Popular Mobilization Units. And ''basij'' is Farsi for ''mobilization.'' So they are cloning structures. And in Syria, they are doing it with the so-called National Defense Forces.

But the big assets really are the Hezbollah-style and Hezbollah-trained militias that operate either in coordination with or under direct control of the Quds Force, bear the IRGC logo, and adhere to the ruling idealogical doctrine that underpins the Islamic regime in Tehran. These are the militias that now effectively control the governments, the Arab capitals.

Now, these Shiite militias also have a new function that had not been present before. They used to be deployed to do terror activities in the past, in the 1980s, as we have discussed, but now they are being used, especially the Iraqi militias, as an expeditionary force that can be sort of sent across borders to advance Iranian interests in neighboring countries like Syria and so on. But there is another aspect to this strategy, that this is not just an expeditionary force. They also look to have their assets dominate state institutions. And this is really a critical point.

There is a synergy now that is growing, especially in Lebanon and Iraq, between Iran's assets and the security forces in both countries. This is a matter of great consequence because the United States has tacitly endorsed this synergy because it is focused on fighting Al Qaeda. So, effectively, we see the Iranians as partners in this fight, and the Iranians have recognized this opening and are exploiting it, positioning themselves as the only viable partners against Sunni extremist groups.

Of course, this is a disastrous policy course for the United States. As things stand today, the Obama administration's partnership with Iran, de facto partnership across the region has resulted in the gradual loss of all commonality with traditional allies.

But Iran's expansionist push, of course, is aimed at targeting these allies and their interests, as we saw in the Golan Heights recently. Iran has set up Hezbollah-Syria down there, and they are looking to set up a new front in the Golan. They are leading, currently, as we speak, an integrated attack pushing into southern Syria, to the borders of Jordan and Israel.

Of course, as Ilan has talked about, this is a global threat. Peru and Uruguay recently—I am sure Ilan will talk about this some more—have caught Hezbollah members and Iranian senior diplomats at their Embassy planning operations.

Yemen stands also as a major problem because it actually has a dual function, on the one hand to pressure Gulf allies, but on the other hand also, by controlling the straits of the Red Sea, this is Iran's preferred smuggling route into Gaza via the Sudan and the Red Sea. So they will then be in charge of the Hormuz Straits and the Bab-el-Mandeb Straits, which makes it a very strategic asset for them.

Now, basically, Washington cannot lose sight of the fact that Iran remains an unreconstructed revolutionary actor, and it cannot just simply be integrated into a new security architecture, as the administration has made it known. And so we need to roll back that influence and disabuse it of this dream of regional hegemony.

There are some steps that we can discuss in the Q&A. I have gone over my limit, so thanks again for the opportunity, and I look forward to taking your questions.

[The prepared statement of Mr. Badran follows:]

Congressional Testimony

State Sponsor of Terror:
The Global Threat of Iran

Tony Badran
Research Fellow, Levant
Foundation for Defense of Democracies

Hearing before House Foreign Affairs Committee
Subcommittee on Terrorism, Nonproliferation, and Trade

Washington, DC
2/11/2015

FOUNDATION FOR
DEFENSE OF DEMOCRACIES   1726 M Street NW • Suite 700 • Washington, DC 20036

Chairman Poe, Ranking Member Keating. Thank you for inviting me to this very timely hearing to testify on the organic relationship between Iran and Hezbollah and the threat they pose to US interests.

Sensing that its moment has arrived, Iran is in the middle of an aggressive region-wide expansionist drive. Today, Iranian officials openly brag about controlling four Arab capitals — Baghdad, Beirut, Damascus and Sanaa. In each of these capitals, the Iranians have developed proxies, either by creating new militias on the Hezbollah model or by coopting pre-existing local actors. They are using these proxies to extend Iran's reach, integrating them into its regional strategy targeting US allies and interests. In each of these capitals, Hezbollah is at the center of Iranian designs.

Since the beginning of the Islamic revolutionary regime in Iran, Hezbollah has enjoyed a privileged place in Iran's regional strategy. Hezbollah was created as an extension of the ruling militant clerical clique and as the long arm of the Islamic Revolutionary Guard Corps (IRGC) in the Arab world. Hezbollah is the first and to date most successful export of the Islamic revolution. From the early 1980's to the present, Hezbollah has been a constant feature of Iranian overseas operations against the US and its allies.

From the outset, the group's progenitors in the IRGC sought to spawn and support militant movements in line with Iran's interests and under its control. But Iran is separated from its Arab surroundings by ethnicity, language and sectarian affiliation. Which is why it invested heavily in Hezbollah. A 1984 statement by Iran's ambassador to Beirut is instructive as to the importance Tehran attached to Hezbollah and Lebanon in its regional strategy: "an Islamic movement [in Lebanon] will result in Islamic movements throughout the Arab world." Indeed, Hezbollah has been instrumental in helping Tehran develop Arab assets and spread its influence across the region. The ability to export its revolutionary model to willing Arab groups allowed Iran to embed itself in Arab societies and project influence, which otherwise would have been far more constrained.

This strategy has arguably reached its peak moment today. Iran's investment in Lebanon is paying dividends like never before since the success of the Islamic revolution. What the Iranians hadn't counted on, however, is that the US would acquiesce to their bid for regional hegemony.

***

When Iranian officials talk about the various regional assets they are supporting in the Arab world, their essential point of reference is Hezbollah. Thus, Ali Akbar Velayati, adviser to Iran's supreme leader Ali Khamenei, recently said to a visiting group of Yemenite clerics in Tehran, "I hope that the [Houthi] Ansar Allah group in Yemen plays a role similar to that of Hezbollah in Lebanon."

Velayati is referring to a specific template that Iran has developed and which it's now establishing in the Arab territories over which it holds sway. In essence, it consists of developing politico-military structures parallel to Arab central governments, especially in countries where those governments are weak. In other words, much like the Soviet Union before it, Iran sets up proxies with the objective of dominating states.

There are several variants of the Hezbollah template. First, there's what Iranian officials call the Basij model, in reference to Iran's paramilitary force. These groups have been established in Iraq, under the name "The Popular Mobilization Forces," as a sectarian volunteer auxiliary to the various Shiite militias and Iraqi Security Forces. Similarly, the Iranians have also encouraged and helped train a parallel phenomenon in Syria, "The National Defense Forces." Describing these forces, the deputy head of the IRGC Lt. Gen. Hossein Salami recently told Fars News Agency, "in Syria, we have a popular army tied to the Islamic Revolution which has chosen the Basiji school of thought as its role model."

On a smaller scale, Hezbollah has cultivated similar groups in Lebanon that serve as its auxiliaries. The war with the Islamic State group (ISIS) has amplified Iran's ability to mobilize these groups and provide them with arms and training. In turn, this expands Tehran's penetration, cements its hold on the weak governments, and increases its influence over the strategic decisions of these states.

But Iran's biggest assets are the militias that, like Hezbollah, are direct extensions of the IRGC. Iran has had longstanding ties to Iraqi Shiite groups that it hosted and sponsored in the 1980's. Some of these groups conducted terrorist activities against Gulf Arab states in the 80's, working in tandem with Hezbollah. Today, these militias, and the multiple spin-offs and splinters that have arisen from them, effectively run southern Iraq. Many of the old faces from the 1980's and 1990's like Abu Mahdi al-Muhandis of Kataib Hezbollah and Hadi al-Amiri of the Badr Organization, are now among the more powerful security figures in Iraq, working directly with Iran's Qods Force commander Qassem Soleimani.

Importantly, these militias are not only operating under the command of the Qods Force, and many bear the IRGC logo, but also most adhere to the ideological doctrine underpinning the Islamic regime in Tehran. As ever, Hezbollah has been central to Iran's effort to train and advise these militias. And whereas Iran deployed these militias in the 1980's and 1990's to conduct terrorist operations against US and allied targets, it now has deployed them in Syria to advance Iranian strategic interests there. This ability highlights the extent of Iran's command and control over these groups and the broader geostrategic theater in which Iran is moving these assets to pursue its objectives.

The IRGC and Hezbollah have also built ties to the Houthi movement in Yemen. Well before the outbreak of the "Arab Spring" in 2011, the Iranians were smuggling weapons by sea to Yemen. As a senior Yemeni security official told Reuters last December, Iranian weapons "are still coming in by sea and there's money coming in through transfers." Hezbollah advisers also came to Yemen to work with the Houthis. When the movement took over Sanaa in September of last year, they freed two Hezbollah operatives that were being held, as well as three IRGC members who were detained when the authorities intercepted an Iranian weapons shipment by sea in January 2013. Support for the Houthis is not only military. Their media arm is operating, with Hezbollah training and assistance, from Beirut where it runs a satellite TV channel.

***

Along with building up alternatives to weak central governments, the Iranian strategy aims to dominate state institutions and dictate these states' overall strategic orientation against traditional US allies in the region.

Hezbollah's domination of the Lebanese government has been evident over the last ten years. Hezbollah's influence over the Lebanese Armed Forces (LAF) has now developed into a synergy. Hezbollah and the LAF might deploy jointly, or the LAF might undertake support operations aiding Hezbollah's war effort against Syrian rebels. In addition, the LAF and other security agencies share with Hezbollah intelligence they receive from the US and other Western states. As such, Hezbollah, a terrorist group, is still able to work hand in glove with the LAF and directly benefit from its legitimacy both domestically and internationally.

The same arrangement exists in Iraq. The Shiite militias now hold sway over the Ministry of Interior. As Eli Lake recently reported from Iraq, "it's increasingly difficult to tell where the Iraqi army ends and the Iranian-supported Shiite militias begin." As with Hezbollah and the LAF, the Iraqi militias are now the beneficiaries of the Iraqi army's international legitimacy and partnership with the US. Consequently, they now operate under US air cover, and help themselves to US-made equipment supplied to the Iraqi army.

This strategy makes Iran and its assets the only viable interlocutors on regional security. Unfortunately, rather than push back, the US appears to be recognizing, if not enabling this new reality.

***

Iran's expansionist push and the cultivation of assets across the region bring pressure on traditional US allies, namely Israel and Saudi Arabia. The recent episode in the Golan Heights serves as a good example.

On January 18, the Israeli army reportedly struck a convoy in the Golan Heights near the town of Quneitra. Riding in the convoy were senior Qods Force and Hezbollah officers, among them Qods Force Brig. Gen. Mohammad Ali Allah-Dadi — Soleimani's man in Syria.

This high-level delegation's presence in the Golan threw into stark relief how Iran's strategy poses a direct threat to US allies and interests. First, the Iranians and Hezbollah had set up "Hezbollah-Syria," which they intended to make a constant feature on the Golan, in order to activate it against Israel. Last April, the conservative Iranian newspaper *Jomhouri Eslami* explained the role "Hezbollah-Syria" would play: "The establishment of Syria's Hezbollah... will also be a strong arm of the resistance that will cause nightmares for the Zionists. The Zionist regime that was concerned about threats from the Lebanese borders, now should prepare itself for a new situation (on the Golan Heights)."

But the threat is not confined to Israel's borders, as Iran and Hezbollah possess global reach. Hence, following the Israeli strike, both the commander of the IRGC, Mohammad Ali Jafari, and Hezbollah chief Hassan Nasrallah, threatened to retaliate "anywhere," "not just in [Israel's] borders, but in any place in the world."

The list of countries in which Iran and/or Hezbollah planned or executed operations against Israeli or Jewish targets in the past few years is long, spanning the entire globe. As such, Jafari's threat is not idle. Last October, Peruvian police arrested Mohammed Amadar, a Hezbollah member who was surveying Israeli and Jewish targets in the Peruvian capital and planning to attack them. Also, reports emerged recently that Uruguay expelled a senior Iranian diplomat in Iran's embassy in Montevideo three weeks ago over his involvement in placing an explosive device near the Israeli embassy in early January. While Uruguay denies expelling the diplomat – who seems to have rather fled the country – this would not have been the first time Iran used its diplomatic corps and missions to conduct terrorist operations abroad – especially in Latin America. The role Iran's "cultural attaché" in Argentina Mohsen Rabbani played in the attacks in Buenos Aires in the 1990's serves as precedent.

Of course, Israel is hardly the only US ally in Iran's crosshairs. The IRGC's agitations in Yemen and Bahrain, to say nothing of Kuwait, testify to Iran's intent to dominate the Gulf and pressure Saudi Arabia. But Yemen in particular affords Iran the additional potential benefit of control over the Red Sea, where Tehran already has longstanding relations in East Africa, especially the Sudan. The Red Sea, of course, is also Iran's established smuggling route to transfer rockets into Gaza. It was in this context that Velayati told the Yemenite delegation in Tehran that "the liberation of Palestine passes through Yemen, which commands a major strategic location."

***

Iran's expansionist drive — as it presses ahead with its nuclear program — represents without question the greatest strategic challenge for the US in the Middle East. Unlike Al-Qaeda, the Iranian network of assets is a state enterprise. What's more, these assets now control weak central governments, allowing them to use these government to obtain the cover of legitimacy. Meanwhile, they subordinate these states to their objectives. This extends beyond using the national armies and security forces, as in Iraq and Lebanon, to making government institutions complicit in terrorist operations, as Hezbollah has done with the Lebanese government. To give an example, Hezbollah has had government-issued passports with false names made for its operatives, as was the case with Mohammad Mansour (a.k.a. Sami Shehab) in Egypt in 2009.

It is therefore imperative for the US to hold the Lebanese government and its Armed Forces accountable. Unfortunately, the US has opted to turn a blind eye to the increased synergy of Hezbollah and the LAF under the pretext of fighting Sunni extremists operating in Syria. The same faulty logic applies in Iraq, where the US is acquiescing to malignant Iranian influence and the dominance of its Shiite militias over the state. Similarly, despite the Houthi group's putsch in Yemen, administration officials have acknowledged maintaining intelligence ties with the Houthis because, as Undersecretary for Defense Michael Vickers recently put it, "they are anti-Al Qaeda."

The Iranians have recognized this opening and are exploiting it, positioning themselves and their assets as the only viable partners against Sunni extremist groups. This is a disastrous policy course for the US. It will push Sunnis, who are revolting against Iranian hegemony in countries like Iraq and Syria, to align with groups like ISIS and Al-Qaeda who present themselves as the vanguards of the fight against Iran and its proxies. Furthermore, aligning closely with Iran and its assets, as they brutalize Sunnis of all stripes, tars the US and alienates all its Sunni allies. The United Arab Emirates withdrawal from the anti-ISIS coalition, citing Washington's acquiescence to a growing Iranian role, should serve as an example of what lies ahead for the US alliance system in the region.

As things stand today, the Obama administration's de facto partnership with Iran across the region has resulted in the gradual loss of all commonality with America's traditional allies. But the US cannot lose sight of the fact that Iran remains an unreconstructed revolutionary, anti-American actor intent on replacing the US as the dominant power in the Middle East. Thirty six years after the Islamic revolution, the ruling clique in Iran is unchanged, as are its ideology, its regional objectives, and the violent tools it has long used to achieve those goals: terrorism, subversion, and setting up militias over which it exerts direct control. For decades, the US policy had been to push back against Iranian subversion in the region, in order to protect the US alliance system in the region. It is time we turn again to that policy, roll back Iran's expansionist drive, and disabuse it of its dreams of regional hegemony.

***

There are several steps that the United States could take to roll back growing regional fears regarding Washington's possible alignment with Iran. Some of them will take the form of reinforcing current administration policies. Some of them will require changes in the administration's current approach to the Middle East.

First, administration officials up to and including the President should make it clear to Iran, to regional allies, and to the global community that US concerns neither begin nor end with Iran's nuclear program. Iran's goal of regional domination and global influence are the overarching threat to American national security. Building a nuclear arsenal is part of that strategy, and a sure means to secure it.

Second, administration officials need to clarify that they understand the links between Sunni radicalism, including and especially in the form of ISIS, and Iranian influence. The United States must make it clear that it understands the enormous degree to which Tehran's influence fuels ISIS. It must to the greatest extent avoid de facto alliances with Iranian proxies in Lebanon, Syria, Iraq, and Yemen. US policymakers will have to adjust how they conduct their operations in the region, and in some cases will have to degrade cooperation with elements otherwise aligned against ISIS.

In Lebanon, assistance to the LAF should be conditioned on the measure of Hezbollah's influence on the institution, and how closely the two work together. Those conditions should be enforced.

In Iraq, we must make it clear to Baghdad that the price for American assistance is genuine inclusiveness with moderate Sunnis, as well as an end to cooperation between Iranian-backed Shiite militias and the Iraqi Security Forces. Other steps may become necessary to rebuild trust in Sunni communities, including dismantlement of the Shiite militias that have been allowed to gain prominence under successive US-backed Iraqi governments.

In Syria, any explicit or implicit coordination with the regime in Syria must be absolutely and totally ended. The objective in Syria needs to be to remove Assad from power, not to legitimize him as a partner.

In Yemen, as our allies have condemned the Houthi coup, any cooperation with the Houthis should be halted at this point.

Congress can play a constructive role in pushing forward these policy goals.

Mr. POE. Dr. Byman?

STATEMENT OF DANIEL L. BYMAN, PH.D., PROFESSOR, SECURITY STUDIES PROGRAM, EDMUND A. WALSH SCHOOL OF FOREIGN SERVICE, GEORGETOWN UNIVERSITY

Mr. BYMAN. Thank you, Mr. Chairman.

And, Mr. Chairman, Ranking Member Keating, and other members of this subcommittee, I appreciate and am honored by the opportunity to testify.

Rather than repeat much of what has been said, which I agree with, I will focus on areas that have not been addressed.

But let me say from the start, I think I have a slightly different view on Iran, which is: Iran can be exceptionally aggressive, but Iran can also be exceptionally weak, it can be cautious, and it is often self-defeating. And we have to look at Iran not only as the aggressive power that it is but, also, at times, as the foolish power that it is, as the weak power that it is.

Iran's military is, I would say, largely pathetic, certainly by Western standards. Its economy is in free-fall. It lacks stature in many countries. And we have to recognize these limits even as we try to combat its support for terrorism.

Let me begin by talking about Syria. The Syrian civil war is a very different sort of thing for Iran and has changed much of what Iran has done historically. First of all, the Syrian civil war, Iran has gone all in. And, from Iran's point of view, this is a tremendous success. It is quite fair to say that without Iranian support Bashar al-Assad might have fallen, and Iran recognizes that.

However, Iran had to lose relations with a number of Sunni allies that it had been working with. And the Palestinian group Hamas, in particular, distanced itself from Iran, although there are incentives on both sides to stay close.

Also, what Iran is doing, what Hezbollah is doing in both Iraq and Syria is actually more akin to counterinsurgency. They are fighting on behalf of governments against rebels. And so, in a way, Iran is in a different role than it often has been historically.

Because of Hezbollah's extensive role in Syria, Hezbollah in general is more cautious about a widespread confrontation with Israel. Hezbollah is overextended. And that certainly doesn't mean there will be no confrontation with Israel, but for Hezbollah it is exceptionally risky, given how much they have invested in the Syria conflict.

Should Iran get a nuclear weapon, which would be a horrible thing, it might exploit that protection and become more aggressive in supporting the groups it supports now and even reach out to others. If it were thwarted, however, through military means, it might use terrorists to take revenge. And, in fact, I think this would be likely. Israel is a particularly likely target of Iranian-backed terrorism.

I would say, under current circumstances, Iran is highly unlikely to do the most extreme forms of terrorism, such as a casualty attack on the 9/11 scale or attacks using unconventional weapons. Nor is Iran likely to transfer a nuclear weapon, if it had one, to a terrorist group. And I can go into my reasons for that should there be interest.

Should there be additional sanctions on Iran in the name of counterterrorism, inevitably they would be seen as sanctions because of the nuclear program. And U.S. allies and Europe, in particular, would have that perception regardless of the justification given in the U.S. context.

In my view, the United States should identify red lines for Iranian behavior, but these red lines need to be things that the administration works with Congress on. There were repeated Iranian violations of U.S. red lines in Iraq, and the United States did nothing. This happened under multiple administrations. And there needs to be consensus before Iran acts so we know how to respond.

And, in particular, I will ask that the United States consider focusing on plots rather than attacks. Just because an attack does not succeed does not mean the intent was not there. And, to me, this is an exceptionally dangerous issue, because, often, attacks don't succeed simply due to bad luck on the part of the attackers.

And I ask, had the attack on the Saudi Ambassador succeeded, had the Saudi Ambassador been killed, had, say, a dozen American diners also been killed, what would the United States have done? And I ask that we think about that now so that we are prepared to respond should there be a similar provocation in the future.

I will also suggest that the United States needs to clarify its Syria policy. Right now, the United States is bombing the enemy of the Assad regime, and it is not surprising that there is a widespread perception in the region that the United States has a deal with Hezbollah, the United States has a deal with Iran. And, regardless, I don't personally think the United States does have that deal, but that perception matters probably more than the reality among many U.S. allies, and that is hurting broader U.S. interests.

I will conclude by saying that, in the end, Iran's lack of strategic options and its general weakness will make it hard to divorce Iran from terrorist groups. It is working with these groups in part because it doesn't have better options, and it is hard to change that. I think better policies can reduce the scope and scale but not eliminate it altogether.

My formal statement goes into these points more extensively, and I thank you for your time today.

[The prepared statement of Mr. Byman follows:]

State Sponsor of Terror: The Global Threat of Iran

Prepared Testimony of Daniel Byman

Professor, Security Studies Program in the Edmund A. Walsh School of Foreign Service
at Georgetown University

Director of Research, Center for Middle East Policy at the Brookings Institution

House Committee on Foreign Affairs
Subcommittee on Terrorism, Nonproliferation, and Trade
February 11, 2015

Chairman Poe, Ranking Member Keating, members of this distinguished subcommittee, and subcommittee staff, thank you for the opportunity to testify today.

Terrorism and support for violent substate movements have long been integral to Iran's foreign policy, making it one of the most dangerous state sponsors of terrorism in the world. Tehran backs terrorism for a wide array of reasons: Iran gains the means to strike around the world, to influence the politics of its neighbors, and to deter the United States and Israel, among other benefits. In a recent shift, Iran is also using its ties to the Lebanese Hizballah and substate groups in Iraq as part of a counterinsurgency effort, working with these groups to bolster the Assad regime in Syria and the Abadi government in Iraq.

Iran could exploit the perceived protection it would gain if it developed a nuclear weapon to step up support for militant groups in the region. If thwarted through military force or other means, Iran might use terrorists to vent its anger and take revenge. Israel is a particularly likely target of Iranian-linked terrorism. However, under current circumstances Tehran still remains unlikely to carry out the most extreme forms of terrorism, such as a mass-casualty attack similar to 9/11 or a strike involving a chemical, biological, or nuclear weapon.

The United States should work with its allies and expand its efforts to counter Iran. However, Iran's behavior is not likely to change significantly: U.S. efforts might reduce Iranian support for terrorism, but they will not eliminate it. The United States should identify and red lines and prepare for action if they are crossed, paying attention to plots – not just successful attacks – and ending the deniability fiction Hizballah sometimes enjoys.

My statement first explains Iran's myriad motivations for supporting terrorist groups. I then describe the level of Iran's current efforts, noting in particular Iran's ties to substate groups in Iraq and Syria as well as recent Iranian-linked plots and attacks. I then assess the dilemma regarding terrorism and Iran's nuclear program. I conclude by presenting implications and recommendations for U.S. policy.[1]

---

[1] This testimony draws extensively on two of my books: *Deadly Connections: States that Sponsor Terrorism* (Cambridge, 2005) and *A High Price: The Triumphs and Failures of Israeli Counterterrorism* (Oxford, 2011). Also relevant to my testimony and to this hearing are my articles, "Iran, Terrorism, and Weapons of Mass Destruction," *Studies in Conflict and Terrorism* Vol. 31 (2008), pp. 169-181; "The Lebanese Hizballah and Israeli Counterterrorism," *Studies in Conflict and Terrorism*, Vol. 34 (2011), pp. 917-941; and Daniel Byman and Bilal Saab, "Hizballah Hesitates," *ForeignAffairs.com*, January 22, 2015.

Iran's Motivations for Supporting Terrorism

Iranian leaders have used terror and terrorism since they took power in 1979. Over 35 years later, Iran continues to use terrorism and work with an array of violent substate groups that use terrorism among other tactics. In his 2014 testimony, Director of National Intelligence (DNI) James Clapper warned that Iran and its ally Lebanese Hizballah continue to threaten U.S. allies and that Hizballah's activity is at a particularly high mark.[2]

Iran's initial motivation for backing terrorist groups was ideological, but this has changed over time. When the Islamic Republic was born in 1979, Ayatollah Khomeini declared that Iran "should try hard to export our revolution to the world."[3] Khomeini's goal is embedded in Iran's constitution and the charter documents of key organizations such as the Islamic Revolutionary Guard Corps (IRGC), a military and paramilitary organization that is in charge of many of Iran's relationships with substate groups.

Iran's closest relationship is with the Lebanese Hizballah, perhaps the most capable terrorist group in the world. Iran helped create Hizballah in the early 1980s, and in subsequent decades has armed and trained it. This assistance is massive: Iran regularly gave Hizballah over $100 million a year, and the figure is often significantly higher. Iran's military aid includes relatively advanced weaponry, such as anti-tank and anti-ship cruise missiles, as well as thousands of rockets and artillery systems, making Hizballah one of the most formidable substate groups in the world. [4]

Hizballah operatives are highly skilled. Iranian intelligence and paramilitary forces work closely with them, often as peers. Politically, Hizballah is loyal to Iran's Supreme Leader, but its own support base in Lebanon and its extensive capabilities give it independence should it choose to use it. However, Hizballah's ideological loyalty and Iran's financial support have kept the two close.

Iran worked with Hizballah to spread revolution in Lebanon, but it also worked with Shi'ite militant groups in Iraq, Bahrain, Pakistan, Afghanistan, and elsewhere, organizing them against rival groups and often against their host governments. After the 1979 revolution, Iran found receptive adherents among embattled and oppressed Shi'ite groups throughout the Muslim world: many Shi'a found Khomeini's charisma and the stunning success of the Iranian revolution inspiring.

Iran's revolutionary fervor has waned as the decades have worn on and as a new set of less-inspiring leaders have come to the fore. Nor do Arab Shi'a look to Iran as a model of revolutionary success given that country's many problems. Tehran increasingly employed terrorists for an array of strategic purposes, and many of these groups are not Shi'a. In Iraq it has worked with an array of Shi'ite factions to try to expand its influence and undercut its rivals. However, Tehran also has ties to Sunni groups including Iraqi Kurdish organizations and Palestine Islamic Jihad. Iran still also has ties to the Palestinian group Hamas, though these are less extensive than in the past. Perhaps most striking, Iran has even allied at times with Al Qaeda and the Taliban even though many members of these groups are violently anti-Shi'a and see Iran's leaders as apostates.

---

[2] James Clapper. "Worldwide Threat Assessment of the U.S. Intelligence Community," January 29, 2014, http://www.intelligence.senate.gov/140129/clapper.pdf, p. 5.

[3] As quoted in Anoushiravan Ehteshami. *After Khomeini* (Routledge, 1995), p. 131.

[4] For a review of Hizballah's international agenda, see Matthew Levitt, *Hezbollah: The Global Footprint of Lebanon's Party of God* (Georgetown, 2013).

Iran's strategic goals for supporting terrorists and other violent substate groups include:

- *Undermining and bleeding rivals.* Iran uses insurgent and terrorist groups to weaken governments it opposes. In the 1980s, this included bitter enemies like Saddam Hussein's Iraq and also lesser foes like the rulers of Kuwait and Saudi Arabia.

- *Power projection.* Tehran's military and economy are weak – and with oil prices plunging and sanctions in place, this weakness is becoming more pronounced. Nor is its ideological appeal strong. Nevertheless, Iran's regime sees itself as a regional and even a world power, and working with terrorists is a way for Iran to influence events far from its borders. Iran's support for the Lebanese Hizballah, Palestine Islamic Jihad, and Hamas make Iran a player in the Israeli-Palestinian and Israeli-Arab disputes, and Iran's backing of Houthis in Yemen give it influence on Saudi Arabia's southern border.

- *Playing spoiler.* Iran has supported groups whose attacks disrupted Israeli-Palestinian and Israeli-Syrian peace negotiations – a victory for Iran, which sees the negotiations as a betrayal of the Muslim cause and as a means of isolating the clerical regime in Iran.

- *Intimidation.* Working with violent substate groups gives Iran a subversive threat, enabling Iran to press its neighbors to distance themselves from the United States or to refrain from joining economic or military efforts to press Iran. Such efforts, however, often backfire: because these states see Iran as meddling in their domestic affairs and supporting violence there, they often become more, not less, willing to support economic or even military pressure directed at Tehran.

- *Deterrence.* Iran's ties to terrorist groups, particularly the Lebanese Hizballah with its global infrastructure, enable it to threaten its enemies with terrorist retaliation. This gives Iran a way to respond to military or other pressure should it choose to do so.

- *Revenge.* Iran also uses terrorism to take revenge. It has attacked dissidents, including representatives of non-violent as well as violent groups, even when they posed little threat to the regime. Iran attacked France during the 1980s because of its support for Iraq, and it has tried to target Israel because of its belief that Israel is behind the deaths of Iran's nuclear scientists and in retaliation for the 2008 killing of Hizballah's operational chief, Imad Mughniyah, which is widely attributed to Israel.[5]

- *Preserving options.* As a weak state in a hostile region, Tehran seeks flexibility and prepares for contingencies. Iran's neighbors have often proved hostile, and rapprochements short-lived. Iran seeks ties to a range of violent groups that give it leverage that could be employed should suspicion turn to open hostility.

Because Iran's approach is now more strategic than ideological, it is willing to work with groups like Al Qaeda, even though mutual mistrust limits cooperation. Many Al Qaeda (and even more Islamic

---

[5] The *Washington Post* reports that the United States was also involved in this killing. Adam Goldman and Ellen Nakashima, "CIA and Mossad killed senior Hezbollah figure in car bombing," *Washington Post*, January 30, 2015, http://www.washingtonpost.com/world/national-security/cia-and-mossad-killed-senior-hezbollah-figure-in-car-bombing/2015/01/30/ebb88682-968a-11e4-8005-1924ede3e54a_story.html

State) supporters loathe Iran, and Sunni jihadists kill Shi'a in Iraq, Pakistan, Afghanistan, and elsewhere with abandon. This hatred has grown as the Syrian civil war has become a sectarian Armageddon. Nevertheless, Iran has worked with Al Qaeda, at times allowing its operatives to transit Iran with little interference. Tehran has also given some Al Qaeda operatives a limited safe haven, though at the same time it often curtails their movements and has even turned some over to the custody of their home governments. Iran's haven is particularly important as the U.S. drone campaign has made Al Qaeda's haven in Pakistan far more dangerous. Iran has also worked with the Taliban, despite almost going to war with it in 1998, in an attempt to keep its options open and at times fight mutual enemies.

Iran gains deniability by working with terrorist groups, though this deniability is often one of willing disbelief on the part of some of its adversaries rather than true uncertainty or confusion. When an Iranian-linked terrorist group carries out an attack, there is always the question of whether Iran ordered it, or even desired it. Even when Iran is determined to be guilty, as was the case with the 1996 Khobar Towers bombing, the time it takes to prove Iran's involvement makes it difficult to gain support for a strong response. However, in many instances this deniability should be highly suspect given the depth of Tehran's ties, its long history with groups like Hizballah, and the fact that many investigations of attacks show involvement at or near the top of Iran's hierarchy.

Iran's Recent Uses of Terrorism and Substate Violence

Iran, often working with Hizballah, has repeatedly tried to use terrorism against an array of Israeli and Western targets and interests, and this pattern has continued in recent years. Recent plots reportedly range from plots against an Israeli shipping company and USAID offices in Nigeria in 2013 to reconnoitering the Israeli embassy in Baku, Azerbaijan, for a possible attack. Hizballah operatives planned an attack in 2014 against Israeli tourists in Bangkok and in October 2014 Hizballah operatives were arrested in Peru for planning attacks against Israeli and Jewish targets there.

The last successful Iranian terrorist attack against the United States outside a theater of war was the 1996 strike on Khobar Towers, which killed 19 Americans. In 2011, the United States disrupted an Iranian plot early in the planning stages to bomb a restaurant in Washington frequented by the Saudi ambassador. Although the target was the Saudi ambassador, the Iranian effort would also probably have killed many U.S. citizens eating at the restaurant.

Attacks on Israel in particular are driven by a mix of aggression and revenge. Iran blames Israel for killing its nuclear scientists, and Hizballah and Israel are engaged in a quiet but deadly struggle in which Israel regularly kills senior Hizballah operatives in Lebanon and Syria, and at times outside this area. For example, in January 2015, Israel reportedly struck Syria and killed Jihad Mughniyeh, the son of Hizballah's operational head and a terrorist in his own right, along with other Hizballah operatives and Iranian paramilitary forces working with them.

Iran has played a major role in backing Bashar al-Assad's regime in Syria and is perhaps the most influential external player in that conflict. Syria is Iran's only Arab ally, and indeed its closest ally in the world, and losing Damascus would be a tremendous blow to Iran's power. Iran's aid spans the spectrum, ranging from troops and training to money and weapons. Hizballah too has deployed thousands of fighters to help the Syrian regime. It is quite possible that Assad's regime would have collapsed without Iranian and Hizballah help, and Iranian officials probably view their efforts in Syria as a tremendous success. However, one price of this success has been a sharp decline in Iran's influence among both Sunni radical groups and Sunni publics, making it harder for Iran to work with Sunni militant organizations and to extend its influence in general.

Similarly, Iran is playing an important role in Iraq, working not only with the Abadi government but also with an array of Shi'ite militias (as well as forces in Iraqi Kurdistan) to fight the Islamic State and other forces.

Iran still retains influence in the Palestinian arena, though less than in the past. After Hamas's founding in 1987, the relationship between Iran and Hamas was polite but limited. Hamas received money, arms, and training from Iran and Hizballah, but Hamas kept Tehran at arm's length, as Hamas leaders were determined to avoid dependence on foreign sponsors, which had often doomed other Palestinian organizations. This relationship became closer after Hamas seized power in Gaza in 2007. Israel, the United States, and the international community tried to isolate Hamas, and it sought both weapons and money: Iran provided both.

The Syrian conflict has frayed Iran's relations with Hamas, though desperation has led both sides to limit the rupture. Hamas sought to position itself on the side of Sunni Arab regimes and Sunnis in general – and thus rejected its longstanding relationship with Assad and, by implication, Assad's backers in Tehran. However, the overthrow of the Muslim Brotherhood regime in Egypt in 2013 and Hamas's repeated conflicts with Israel have left Hamas isolated and in need of international friends. Iran seeks to avoid losing all ties to Sunni groups, making Hamas particularly valuable. Iran also has close ties to the smaller Palestine Islamic Jihad, a rival to Hamas though a less powerful organization.

Hizballah is probably less eager to renew the struggle with Israel at this point despite its continued hostility. Hizballah makes limited responses against Israeli attacks on its operatives in Syria, and it still seeks revenge for the killing of Imad Mughniyeh. However, its forces are deeply engaged in Syria: a demanding war, and one that has greatly decreased Hizballah's popularity among non-Shi'a in Lebanon and made it enemy number one for Sunni jihadists. Although attacking Israel is part of Hizballah's raison d'être and Hizballah might gain some support for doing so, the group is overstretched, and it would be difficult for the group to sustain several large wars at once. Hizballah in general has been quiet against Israel since the 2006 conflict, and it has a healthy respect for Israel's military and the damage Israel would do to Lebanon and Hizballah should there be another war.

The United States, Iran, and Hizballah are all engaged in counterinsurgency (and in some ways in counterterrorism) in the fight against the Islamic State and like-minded groups in Iraq and Syria (and, in Hizballah's case, supporters of these groups operating in Lebanon). Although U.S. officials are adamant that there is no formal cooperation between U.S. forces and the IRGC or Hizballah, the United States does coordinate with the Lebanese government and especially the Iraqi government – and both of these coordinate with Iran and have militaries and security forces that Iranian intelligence has probably penetrated extensively. So de facto coordination, or at least deconfliction of operations, is likely occurring.

The Nuclear Dilemma

Iran's nuclear program complicates the counterterrorism dilemma. Israel's efforts to disrupt Iran's program and fight terrorism have led to a shadow war between the two countries, creating a retaliatory dynamic. Iranian leaders both desire revenge and seek to prove to their domestic audiences (particularly the IRGC) that Iran will not be humiliated, so they use terrorism to go after Israeli targets around the world as well as to carry out cross-border attacks.

It is too recent to draw firm conclusions, but Iran's use of extra-regional terrorism directly against the United States appears to have declined since negotiations over Iran's nuclear program began in earnest. Iran has not repeated any plot similar to the 2011 attack on the Saudi ambassador to the United States; the 2013 Nigeria arrest is worrisome, but that occurred before negotiations became serious, and publicly available information is incomplete in any event. DNI Clapper's public testimony in 2014 stressed the danger Iran's terrorism posed to U.S. allies, not the U.S. homeland.

A military strike by Israel or the United States on Iran would probably prompt a more massive terrorism response. Tehran backs terrorist groups in part to keep its options open: now it would call in its chits. Iran would probably attempt attacks around the world, using its own operatives, the Lebanese Hizballah, and other groups. Tehran would also step up activity against U.S. forces in Afghanistan and Iraq, using its proxies and perhaps its own paramilitary forces to conduct attacks. The scope and scale of the Iranian response would depend on the level of casualties from the initial attack against it as well as the political circumstances of the regime in Tehran (and those of strong groups like Hizballah) at the time the attack occurred. However, Iran would be likely to attempt multiple attacks and would consider strikes on the American homeland as well as on American diplomatic, military, and civilian institutions worldwide.

An Iran with a nuclear weapon would be a more dangerous force in the region, and preventing this should be a priority for any U.S. administration.[6] A nuclear weapon probably would embolden Iran. Currently, the threat of a U.S. conventional military response limits Iran's aggressiveness, but a nuclear weapon would enable Iran to deter a U.S. conventional strike. Iran could then become more aggressive supporting Hizballah, various opposition forces to Arab regimes, Palestinian terrorist groups, and more extreme forces in Iraq. Iran could become more like Pakistan: after Islamabad acquired nuclear weapons, it gained a shield from India's conventional superiority and became more aggressive in backing anti-India substate groups.

Iran, however, would probably not transfer a nuclear weapon to a terrorist group unless the circumstances were extreme. Too much could go wrong if Iran passed such a sensitive capability to a group, and Tehran's policies in the post-revolutionary period have not been that risky. Iran knows that the United States and Israel would see such a move as exceptionally provocative and would dramatically escalate efforts against Iran – and that they would likely gain the support of all major powers, as even Beijing and Moscow fear such transfers given their own considerable terrorism problems. Deniability would go out the window, as even the possibility of such a move would be alarming. A sign of Iran's caution is that it has not transferred chemical weapons to Hizballah despite having had these in its arsenal for decades. Indeed, Hizballah does not seek unconventional weapons (it could have easily produced chemical weapons on its own) and is not seeking to escalate unconventionally against Israel or the United States.

Should Iran fear invasion and regime change, however, this calculus might change. Iran might transfer weapons as a deterrent, as a way of saving some capacity from a preemptive strike, or simply out of revenge.

Policy Implications and Recommendations

U.S. policy can and does reduce Iran's use of terrorism, but there are limits. The United States should continue to work with its allies to fight Iranian-backed terrorism. This is particularly problematic when it comes to Hizballah, as U.S. allies often look the other way at Hizballah activities in their countries because the group also engages in "legitimate" political and social welfare activity. A strongly enforced ban on any support for Hizballah in any form would create an incentive for the Lebanese

---

[6] It is difficult to predict how Iran would behave with a nuclear weapon, and some scholars are relatively optimistic. See most prominently Kenneth N. Waltz, "Why Iran Should Get the Bomb," *Foreign Affairs* (July/August 2012), http://www.foreignaffairs.com/articles/137731/kenneth-n-waltz/why-iran-should-get-the-bomb

organization to reduce its use of violence. Allies should also be encouraged to reduce the size of Iranian diplomatic missions and otherwise make it harder for Iranian intelligence operatives to act freely.

Pressing Iran to reduce or stop its support for terrorism is difficult, however, in part because of the efforts over the nuclear program. The U.S. sanctions campaign – to include sanctions currently in place and those measures that have been suspended while negotiations go on – is already focused on Iran's nuclear program. There is a limited amount that could be added, and any new sanctions would inevitably be seen (in both Iran and the United States) as linked to Iran's nuclear program, even if done in the name of counterterrorism. U.S. allies in Europe would perceive such a move as undermining negotiation efforts on Iran's nuclear program.

An agreement that prevents Iran from getting a nuclear weapon would benefit counterterrorism. Iran would not be able to use a nuclear weapon as a shield from U.S. conventional pressure, and its terrorist proxies would be less likely to be emboldened.

The United States should also set clear "red lines" regarding Iranian behavior. This includes the transfer of unconventional weapons to a terrorist group or any strike on the U.S. homeland or U.S. facilities. For example, was it clear what the U.S. response would have been had the plot against the Saudi ambassador succeeded? Administration officials, in consultation with Congressional leaders, should decide in advance where the red lines are and what would happen if a red line were crossed, and have the will and ability to follow through on the response should this happen. During both the George W. Bush and Obama administrations, Tehran repeatedly crossed U.S. red lines in Iraq and Afghanistan with relatively few consequences, reducing the credibility of future U.S. threats. If the United States is not serious about a response, it is better not to threaten at all.

In addition, the United States should focus on *plots* rather than *attacks* when gauging the intensity of Iranian-backed terrorism. The success or failure of a terrorist attack often involves tactical skill by intelligence services and a degree of luck: we cannot assume that success today means success tomorrow, and counterterrorism officials regularly warn of just such a possibility. For terrorism, it is the intent that should matter and policy should be focused accordingly. Thus the plot against the Saudi ambassador should have been treated as if it had succeeded, and future anti-U.S. plots should be treated with all seriousness even if they are foiled.

The United States should also take advantage of the growth in sectarianism and the brutality of the Islamic State to try to sever Iranian ties to Sunni jihadists in general. Tehran has largely gotten a free pass on the Al Qaeda presence within its borders: if it were widely publicized, this presence would be embarrassing to both Tehran and the Sunni jihadists, and an information campaign could harm this cooperation.

The United States needs clarity in its Syria policy in particular. In Iraq, the United States can work with Sunni tribes, the Iraqi government forces (such as they are), and the Kurdish *peshmerga* in the fight against the Islamic State, and U.S. efforts so far have attained some success. Iranian paramilitary forces and Iran-linked groups are also fighting the Islamic State, but the United States can fight the Islamic State without them. Syria is a tougher nut. The moderate Syrian opposition is weak and getting weaker. The Assad regime – and its allies, Iran and Hizballah – is of course an effective enemy of the Islamic State, but the United States seeks the Assad regime's downfall, and allying with it is morally noxious and would alienate many U.S. regional allies. So the United States is in an uneasy position of opposing Iran and Hizballah's role in Syria even though they are among the most effective means of fighting the Islamic State there. Not surprisingly, many observers believe that the United States is tacitly aligned with Iran and Hizballah because we are all fighting the same enemy in Syria and Iraq.

The fall of the Assad regime in Syria is desirable and would reduce Iran's influence, but it would not dramatically change Tehran's support for terrorism and may even increase Iran's reliance on substate groups. Although Hizballah would lose an important patron should the regime in Damascus change, and it would be harder for Iran to ship weapons to Lebanon via Syria, the importance of Hizballah would grow for Iran. It remains relatively easy to send weapons to Lebanon without transiting Syria, and Hizballah's role in the Lebanese government (and control of Beirut's airport) makes it almost impossible to stop the flow of weapons there. So Iran may end up doubling down on substate groups if it loses its main regional ally. The explosive growth of the Islamic State and jihadists in general in the region further complicates U.S. policy in Lebanon, as a decline in Hizballah influence there might increase the strength of jihadists rather than more moderate pro-Western Lebanese voices.

In the end, Iran's lack of strategic options and desire to respond to what it sees as a hostile world will lead Tehran to continue to work with a range of terrorist groups and selectively use violence. Successful U.S. policy can reduce the scope and scale of Iranian violence, but it is not likely to end it altogether.

Mr. POE. Thank you, gentlemen.

The subcommittee will be in recess until after the series of two votes, so we will be in recess until then. We are adjourned. Maybe three votes.

[Recess.]

Mr. POE. The subcommittee will come to order. I would ask one of the people on the very back row, if you would shut the backdoor, I would appreciate it.

Thank you, gentlemen, for returning, assuming that you may have never left. Thank you for your insightful testimony. It was excellent.

I want to start with Yemen and the country of Yemen, a supporter, generally, of the United States. Yemen—good relationship. Are the Iranians responsible for the overthrow of the government?

Anybody? You all have an opinion, I know.

Mr. KAGAN. I will take it.

So, at Critical Threats, we have been tracking Yemen very, very closely, and we have an analyst looking at this full-time.

I don't think that the Iranians are responsible for the overthrow in the sense that I don't think they ordered it and I don't think that they intended for it to happen. I think that Iranian strategy in Yemen was, as has been described by all of the witnesses and everyone on the panel, about getting their tentacles into the government, getting effective control without responsibility for elements of the security service. I don't think that they intended to sponsor a coup d'etat.

It is not entirely clear to me that the Houthis intended to stage a coup d'etat either. They did, effectively, and we should call things by their right names. But I think that they may have gotten there by having their bluff called by President Hadi in a way that turned a power play into a coup d'etat. I think that is possible.

But are the Iranians supporting the Houthis? Absolutely. Are they supporting them in this play? Yep. Will they continue to support them? You bet.

Mr. POE. And, Mr. Berman? Different answer?

Mr. BERMAN. I defer to Tony.

Mr. POE. Mr. Badran?

Mr. BADRAN. Oh, I am sorry. I wasn't——

Mr. BERMAN. No, no, no.

Mr. POE. One of you. Mr. Badran. I am going to pick a horse and ride it. Mr. Badran?

Mr. BADRAN. Okay.

Well, just to add to what Dr. Kagan said, that now that this has happened, the Iranians are not hiding the lofty plans that they have for the Houthis and how they want to integrate them into their broader network in the region. So you have posters of the Houthi leader in Tehran with writings, you know, that the revolution, i.e. The Islamic Revolution, continues. And so they see it as an extension of their own vision and network of alliances in the region.

And, recently, a Web site affiliated with the IRGC laid down what it hopes to see done by the Houthis. And it is exactly what I have described, this template that I was talking about. They advised them to create Popular Mobilization Units. They advised them to integrate with the military forces so that you will have the same system that you have in Lebanon, that you have in Iraq, whereby you have an asset, an Iranian asset, or ally, in this case, shaping the military security and intelligence and broader strategic orientation of the state in which they are operating. So I think that is what they want.

And I mentioned—I am not sure if I mentioned in my openings remarks that Velayati, Khomeini's consigliere, as it were, recently received a delegation of Yemenite Houthi clerics in Tehran and again also said to them that he hopes that they play the role of Hezbollah in Lebanon.

So they have their plans, and they see also—you know, he even had a statement about how the road to the liberation of Palestine will pass through Yemen and so on. So, I mean, they have big, big plans, I think, for the Houthis.

Now, whether the Houthis end up not having much of a choice but to go along with these or whether they pull back remains to be seen, I think.

Mr. POE. You mentioned in your testimony that they were in different—Hezbollah and Iran—sponsor of terrorism was in—or maybe it was Dr. Kagan—they are in every continent except Antarctica. One of you said that. Which one of you said that?

You don't remember? One of you said it.

You think you did?

Okay. Well, how many countries are they involved in? If you could be a little more specific.

Mr. BADRAN. Right.

Mr. POE. In your analysis, you all's analysis, world sponsor of terrorism—state sponsor of terrorism, how many countries is Iran, with its affiliate Hezbollah or some other affiliate, involved in terror, mischief, if I can use that phrase?

Mr. BADRAN. I think one way to look at it—and this is not comprehensive—one way to look at it is, wherever there is a Shia, especially Lebanese Shia, population—for instance, in West Africa—that gives them an opportunity, gives them a pool of recruits. Same thing applies to South America, where there is a large Lebanese constituency. So then they latch onto that.

And since Hezbollah now is really the dominant force among the Lebanese Shia, that extends into these areas. So the guy, for instance, that the Peruvian police arrested in October had a Sierra Leonean passport. Sierra Leone is where a lot of Lebanese Shia expats live and control much of the business. Nigeria, same thing. And that is where you had an operation that the Iranians were involved in with arms trafficking.

So they sit at the nexus of these things, in whatever they can procure money, weapons, smuggling, or recruit operatives. So I will stop at this particular angle, but I am sure——

Mr. POE. So they are opportunists. They take the opportunity, when a situation in a particular country meets their needs because of the local population, that they get involved.

How many countries would that be? That is really my question. Just give me a ballpark figure. Somebody.

Mr. BERMAN. I would just chime in here at this point and say that I think it is difficult to come up with anything resembling an accurate tally, because what you have, in many instances, are moments in time——

Mr. POE. Okay.

Mr. BERMAN [continuing]. Sort of impressionistic events. For example, in Thailand and in New Delhi in 2012, when you had the attempted terrorist attacks on the Israeli persons of interest and targets, it wasn't clear that there was a longstanding, established Hezbollah or IRGC cell, but it was clear that, for that particular operation, it was operating in those countries.

That makes it difficult to quantify exactly what size the global footprint is. But it is clear that, where there is empty political space, as there is in Latin America, where there is economic opportunity and the opportunity to exploit gray and black markets, as there is in Asia, the IRGC is very heavily involved, and, to a lesser extent, so is Hezbollah.

Mr. POE. One more question regarding that issue. Where does Iran get the money to be the state sponsor of terror that it is, to pay for all of these operations? Whether they be a moment in time or whether they be long-term, where do they get the money?

Mr. BYMAN. Mr. Chairman, part of why Iran sponsors terrorism is it is relatively cheap compared to other alternatives.

It gives a lot of money to the Lebanese Hezbollah. So you can cite any figure you want, but let's say several hundred million a year. But in the vast majority of other cases, we are talking low millions, we are talking often single-digit personnel. And if you compare that to the cost of, say, you know, having a brigade in a combat zone, it is peanuts.

So, in a strange way, this is a way of saving money rather than spending money, the exception, though, being Lebanon in the past and I would say Syria, in particular, today, where Iran is pouring I have no idea how much, but it is, I would say, in the high hundreds of millions, billions. I am not sure of the exact figure.

Mr. POE. So they get more bang for their buck. Even probably with the cost of developing the nuclear weapons, they can go and commit specific acts of terror for a lot less money.

Mr. BYMAN. I would put nuclear weapons and terrorism on, kind of, two ends of a spectrum, where terrorism gives you lots of local capabilities, lots of ways to do small-scale things, and, of course, a nuclear weapon is the other extreme.

Mr. BADRAN. The other aspect, also, is when you have a group like Hezbollah that has gotten into a position of prominence in the Lebanese state, it gives them opportunities to exploit corruption and other ventures within the Lebanese state to make money—racketeering, drug trade, weapons smuggling, and so on and so forth.

And then when you latch on the extra layer of Lebanese Shiite businessmen, very well-to-do, in Latin America, West Africa—for instance, in Angola, the Treasury Department has designated a Shia businessman, three brothers actually, vastly—the Tajideen brothers—very successful. They are all Hezbollah operatives, right? So a lot of these guys they can either extort money from or just simply incorporate into their financial networks.

So there are multiple revenues that they can actually draw on.

Mr. POE. Thank you.

I will yield to the ranking member, Mr. Keating.

Mr. KEATING. Thank you, Mr. Chair.

Given the apparent opposite positions on the civil conflict in Syria, what is your assessment of the current state of relations with Iran and Hamas? And to what extent did Iran back Hamas in the July 2014 conflict with Israel?

Mr. BADRAN. I think, in many respects, that war was Hamas's way of reorienting its ship back to Iran.

The Iranians have been able to sort of get beyond the political leadership of Hamas, Khaled Meshaal and all these guys that broke with Syria and broke with the axis once the Syrian revolution broke out, and reach directly to the military commanders. So now you have a lot of more prominence of the Qassam Brigade commanders and the various other—Islamic Jihad, for instance, got its profile heightened as a result of Hamas's abandonment of Bashar.

Although, now, they are right on the, sort of, road to penance back to Tehran. And you hear a lot of reports about impending visits to Tehran by Khaled Meshaal, for instance. And, ironically, it is actually Bashar al-Assad who is saying, no, not yet, he has to pay for it some more, he has to beg some more, he has to be made to pay for his sins some more.

So I think the Iranians—Hamas knows that neither Turkey nor Qatar, nobody else can actually replace Tehran as a source of firepower for them. So they don't have a choice; they are going to maintain that relationship.

Mr. KEATING. Okay.

Mr. BERMAN. Sir, if I may, I was actually in Israel right at the tail end of the 50-day Gaza war last year, and I had very interesting conversations with a number of Israeli officials, who made the point of telling me that what had happened was essentially a strategic tie, that Hamas had gained something in terms of renewed ideological relevance and legitimacy, but that Israel had gained something, too, because it had managed to erode Hamas's stockpile of short-range rockets; it had managed, sort of, to go into Gaza and hollow out the arsenal.

The reality is, I think, that the proper context to understand the Gaza war is as a bid for continued relevance on the part of Hamas. If you look at what had happened in the months preceding, Hamas had found itself unexpectedly the junior partner in this hybrid Palestinian Authority unity government that Mahmoud Abbas had proposed, and their funding stream had dried up from Iran because Hamas and Iran had essentially fallen out over Syria, and Hamas had had its budget zeroed out, effectively. The end result was that Hamas had to rely on sponsors like Turkey, like Qatar to pay salaries, for example, in the Gaza Strip.

That is not the case today. What you are seeing today is a renewed closeness of ties between Hamas and Tehran, animated by Hamas's being able to prove itself as a vanguard of the Palestinian resistance, as they would term it, but also by interest from Iran in regaining some of the ground in the Sunni world that it has lost over the last 3 years because it has supported Bashar al-Assad's Syria in a way that has alienated its traditional allies or at least its traditional partners.

Mr. KEATING. We have made a lot about the commonality of Iran and U.S. in terms of ISIS. But there are reports that have surfaced about—leave it that way—about the brutality of the Shia militia from Iran, not only going after ISIS but then, given the opportunity, just brutally attacking Sunni tribes. And, of course, in the big picture, that creates an enormous problem, you know, for any kind of success in the long run.

Do you want to comment on that aspect of their actions?

Mr. KAGAN. I would love to.

I think that the commonality of interest with Iran over ISIS is greatly exaggerated. We have an interest in separating ISIS from the Sunni community and bringing the Sunni community back into polities of which it has historically been a part in Iraq and Syria and elsewhere.

Iran, whatever their statements, tends to see the Sunni community as ISIS, and their militias certainly treat them in that way. So the reports of brutality and mass executions and mass graves in Diyala province are well-documented, but even, in addition to that, one of the reasons Baghdad is relatively secure now is because the Shia militias went into a small area called Jurf al-Sakher, southwest of Baghdad, which was a Sunni area and has long been an AQI and now ISIS support, and they just moved everybody out. They just took the entire Sunni population and moved them out. And they have no plans to bring them back.

And that fact came up repeatedly in discussions that I had in Baghdad, with Sunni leaders and others saying, you know, you want the Sunni community to work with Baghdad, but, you know, the example is Jurf al-Sakher. So this is definitely much more of a problem than any commonality in interest we might have.

Mr. KEATING. Yeah. Well, thank you.

I yield back.

Mr. POE. I thank the gentleman from Massachusetts.

The Chair recognizes the gentleman from New York, Mr. Higgins, for his questions.

Mr. HIGGINS. Thank you very much, Mr. Chairman, for holding this important hearing.

I just kind of want to explore the role of Qasem Soleimani. You know, we have read in the last several months about him. He is probably the most influential force in the Middle East, not necessarily for good, right now—in Iraq, in Syria, in south Lebanon with Hezbollah.

I am interested in your thoughts about him, and his influence embellished or is that an accurate description of his outsized influence?

Mr. KAGAN. Well, he is, in fact, extremely important. He does work directly to the Supreme Leader. We call it the IRGC Quds Force. There is the notion that he is subordinated to the IRGC commander, General Jafari. In reality, I do not believe that he is actually subordinated. He does work directly to the Supreme Leader, and they have a very close relationship.

And Soleimani has bragged to American commanders in the region about how he is their opposite number and how he is in control of things. And there is a lot of bravado there, but he clearly is in control of a lot of the military operations that are going on in Iraq and Syria, especially by militia elements.

One of the things that our team has been observing, however, that is very interesting is that there has been a conscious and deliberate campaign by IRGC senior commanders over the past several months to build him up, and it has become a mayor regime PR objective to establish him as a major figure. We are still noodling what that is about. It is not entirely clear what the regime or this element of it intends to accomplish.

But he is definitely dominant in the region, but there is also a campaign to make him seem even more significant than he might be.

Mr. BERMAN. If I could add just 10 seconds on what Dr. Kagan said, I think that is exactly right.

It is necessary to understand Soleimani in the two constituencies in which he moves. The first is the external one, in which he is a fixer and he is sort of a jack of all trades in Iraq and, to some extent, in Syria, as well. He has famously boasted to General Petraeus when Petraeus was in charge of U.S. Forces in Iraq that he was his opposite number, that he was in control of Iranian policy, not only in Iraq but also in Afghanistan and in Syria.

But the messaging campaign that you see coming out of the regime now—and it is, by the way, broader than just the IRGC. It looks very much like a public diplomacy push on the part of the Iranian regime. It has cast Soleimani in the light of a savior of the Islamic republic.

Because one of the things, I believe, that the regime is trying to do is to rally public opinion around Iran's expeditionary forces. And the perfect target of that is ISIS. Soleimani is now at the tip of the spear in the Iranian fight against ISIS, and he is being perceived more and more not like a knight-errant on the part of the Supreme Leader but as a champion for the regime itself. It is one that has, I think, rebounded to the benefit of the stature of the IRGC writ large within Iran itself.

Mr. BADRAN. Just very quickly, also, in this particular angle in southern Syria, the recent strike that the Israelis did there targeted a major general in the Quds Force that actually was brought in by Soleimani, so he is very much seen as Soleimani's guy in Syria.

In addition, it targeted Jihad Mughniyeh, Imad Mughniyeh's son. Jihad Mughniyeh, there are a couple of stories about him. One was that he was living as a playboy in Beirut, and the party, because of the importance of his name and the legacy of his father, took him and shipped to Tehran, where, actually, Soleimani took him under his wing. And you will see a lot—at the funeral of Soleimani's mother, Jihad Mughniyeh was right by his side, and he was kind of seen as his protege, probably being groomed for some future role. And the fact that he was with Soleimani's man in southern Syria suggests that they had a lot of plans for him as that.

But, as Dr. Kagan and Berman have said, basically there is a huge information operation that the Quds Force is running, with Qasem Soleimani popping up in pictures everywhere on every front, including, now, supposedly in southern Syria as they are making a push to the south. Nobody knows if it is real or not; it is just that they want to put his face that he is on the front line, Iran is on the front line through Qasem Soleimani on every front, both with the Israelis and with ISIS, in the region.

Mr. BYMAN. Sir, I will only briefly add that, although we focus a lot on Soleimani, the Quds Force, the IRGC, they report to the Supreme Leader. They reflect Iranian policy. Policies are coordinated. They are quite good at what they do, and they also are given some freedom to act. But, in general, we always need to remember this is Iranian policy rather than, necessarily, Quds Force policy.

Mr. HIGGINS. I am out of time.

Mr. POE. I don't use this word very often, but I will be liberal with the time if you have another question or two.

Mr. HIGGINS. Well, the recent Shia militia victory over ISIS in Iraq by the Badr organization—who is the primary influence in the Badr organization?

Mr. KAGAN. So the Badr organization is commanded by Hadi al-Amiri, who is an Iraqi. He is a subordinate, basically, of Qasem Soleimani, along with another Iraqi, nominally, named Muhandis, who is the leader of the Kata'ib Hezbollah militia, and he is also a subordinate of Soleimani.

Mr. HIGGINS. If Congress authorizes the President to commit ground troops in Iraq, aren't we entering into a similar situation that we entered into in 2003?

I mean, it is not as though, you know, American troops would just be fighting ISIS, which—it is estimated there are some 30,000 fighters, which I still don't quite understand, and anybody who looks at it rationally should question this.

You have the Peshmerga, which is 190,000 fighters proven to be Western/United States allies, proven to be reliable, proven to be experienced. You have the Iraqi National Army; let's say conservatively it is another 175,000. And you have the Shia militias. And then you have, you know, an estimated 31,000 ISIS fighters. We should be—the math doesn't add up to a situation that we have right now, where ISIS is still dominant in that country.

And my sense is that Soleimani will be using these Shia militias to fight both ISIS and the United States, because that is their history. And the bottom line is, for the second term of Nouri al-Maliki, Soleimani cut the deal not in Baghdad but in Tehran. And, you know, the consensus was that we will all be part of this bad deal under one condition, that the Americans leave.

I am just very concerned about what happens if we commit ground troops, even on a limited basis, to Iraq to fight ISIL because we will be fighting other forces that we fought previously, as well. That is my last thought.

Mr. KAGAN. If I could respond to that?

Mr. HIGGINS. Sure.

Mr. KAGAN. It is a very legitimate concern. And I think that it is quite possible that a significant American presence in Iraq could be targeted by Iranian militias. But I am a bit more concerned about what is likely to happen if we don't involve ourselves and if we don't offer the Iraqis an alternative.

I would not be supportive of sending American troops into Diyala. That is controlled by Badr; it is controlled by Soleimani.

The Iraqi Army unit there is infiltrated. But our general assessment is that there are Iraqi units in Anbar, in Ninawa, elsewhere, that are not controlled by the Iranians and that don't want to be controlled by the Iranians and that want to have an alternative.

And I would submit, this isn't really about ground forces versus not ground forces. I mean, we have boots on the ground there now. You know, we don't say that, but that is—they have boots, and they are on the ground. We are in it. And I think we have had a positive impact.

I think we need to continue in a way that makes it clear to the Iraqis that they can have one set of advisors at any given moment. They can have Iranian advisors, or they can have American advisors. And that goes unit by unit. I think that you will find that, in a lot of places, they will prefer to have American advisors because we can bring a lot more to the table if we choose.

Now, the Iranians will resist that. Will they attack us? I don't know. There is a lot that goes into that calculous. And, of course, they can attack us anyway if we are in the region.

But I think that we need to be very cognizant of the danger of being absent from this conflict in such a way that we give the Iraqis proof when they say, ''Hey, the Iranians are here, and you are not. You know, what do you want us to do?''

Mr. BADRAN. There is another concern I think that we have to keep in mind, is that there is a reason why the United States has failed to recruit significant Sunni tribes to fight this fight. And the reason ISIS's power is so magnified is not because of how many people it has; it is because of the alliances that it has among the Sunni tribes.

And the reason why it is capable to have this alliance is because of the nature of Iranian influence in the Baghdad government and the security forces, Ministry of Interior in particular. The Badr organization is very strong in the Ministry of Interior. In fact, the head of the Ministry of Interior is very much a subordinate of Hadi al-Amiri that Dr. Kagan mentioned.

And so I think, once the—this is what I talked about in my testimony in terms of the synergy or the fusion between the Shiite militias on the one hand and the central government and how it completely complicates our ability when it comes to the Sunnis, both on partnering with the Sunnis and on defeating Sunni radical groups like ISIS.

So I think the perception of us coming into Iraq sort of shoulder-to-shoulder with a very dubious, penetrated central government to fight Sunnis is going to harm, I think, our alliances with a lot of Sunnis unless we, sort of, really leverage our interference to review how we deal with the Baghdad government and what the nature of the Baghdad government is.

Mr. POE. I thank the gentleman from New York.

The Chair will now recognize one of our new members, Ms. Kelly from Illinois, for her questions.

Ms. KELLY. Thank you, Mr. Chair.

I want to thank the committee and the witnesses for the opportunity to have this important discussion today.

I just came from the House floor, and we had a moment the silence for Kayla Mueller. And her death is a real reminder to us of all the challenges that we face in this world.

As we discuss global threats and Iran, I wanted to ask, how do you see Iranian objectives in Iraq different than the United States objectives?

Mr. KAGAN. Well, I think the Iranians have a number of very clear objectives, and one of them that is in conflict is their objective is to get us out and keep us out forever, and our objective is, or should be, to continue to play some role. And I am not talking here about military. I am talking about influence—political, economic, and so forth.

The Iranians very much would like Iraq to be subordinate to them, loyal to them, or at least hostile to us, and they have been working hard to make that happen. They are determined to ensure that there is a Shia government in power in Baghdad and that the Sunni are marginalized, because they see the Iraqi Sunni largely as a threat. And they have a number of other objectives with regard to the Kurds where we may or may not be a little bit crossed.

But the most important conflict in our interest is not just in Iraq but it is around the region. The Iranians are very explicit about this in their statements and their actions. Their objective is to eject us from the Middle East entirely. That is their goal. And they work on making that happen. Our objective is to remain engaged in a region that is of critical strategic importance.

Ms. KELLY. Uh-huh.

Mr. KAGAN. As long as those interests are crossed in that way, we are going to be having problems.

Ms. KELLY. Did you want to——

Mr. BERMAN. Just to add a layer of complexity to what Dr. Kagan said, I think it is necessary to understand Iran's objectives in Iraq through prism of ideology as well.

When the Ayatollah Khomeini swept to power in Tehran 36 years ago this month, he was both the rahbar, the political leader of the Islamic republic, and the marja taqlid, the ideological religious model of emulation.

The current Supreme Leader was a consensus candidate that emerged in 1989 after Khomeini's death. He is superceded in the hierarchy of Shiite theology by a number of clerics, most importantly a gentleman by the name of Ali Sistani, who is an Iraqi cleric.

So, when we talk in the context of what Iran wants in Iraq, the question of Iraqi independence is not just about Iraqi political independence; it is also about Iraq's ideological independence. Because an independent Iraq that is capable of embracing the quietest tradition that Sistani espouses will be both an ideological and a political threat to Iran. So Iran's objectives in Iraq are not only to keep us out but to keep other interpretations of Shiite Islam down.

Mr. BYMAN. I will add only briefly that Iran also wants a weak Iraq and is comfortable with a low level of instability. Iran does not want the scale of violence that is happening in Iraq now, but they are much more comfortable with the low level because it makes the Iraqis dependent on Iran, and they are quite pleased with that. So some degree of strife and keeping Iraq off balance, in a way, serves the Iranian goals that Dr. Kagan identified.

Ms. KELLY. Where do you see Iran's influence in Iraq? Like, where is it strongest, and where is it weakest?

Mr. BYMAN. What the Iranians are very good at, of course, is working with an array of Shia groups. And they have very good ties to the main government, to the Abadi government.

However, Iran hedges its bets. So it works with groups, Shia groups, that at times shoot at each other. And it works with violent ones; it works with more moderate ones. It also works with an array of Kurdish groups. It has reached out to some of the crazy Sunni groups that would happily kill a Shia if they saw one. So Iran is almost painfully pragmatic in its willingness to work with groups.

Its influence is strongest, I would say, certainly in the Shia areas. Also, it has a lot of local influence along its border. Iran looks at Iraq not just as a country but as a series of regions and cities and towns, and it tries to buy influence at the local level, as well.

Ms. KELLY. Anyone else?

Mr. KAGAN. I think that Iran's influence varies. I think, overall, Iran's influence in Iraq is higher than it has ever been. But it does vary, and it is changing, and interesting things are going on, primarily, I would say, because of the degree to which the Iranian-backed militias have effectively shown that they are completely independent of the Iraqi political leadership and actually are acting just as subordinates of Soleimani.

And that has had the effect of scaring the Shia political leadership in Iraq about these militias and about what the Iranians are actually trying to do. Does it reduce Iranian influence? You know, not necessarily. But it has created, I would say, a different atmosphere in which that influence is received.

And, again, I think, frankly, it is an opportunity for us, because Hadi al-Amiri and Muhandis have shown their hands, and they have shown Iran's hand also, much more than they have in the past, not in terms of their activities, because they are not doing much that is very different from what they have done before, but in terms of their posturing.

And it is interesting to see—Muhandis is a guy who was always a shadowy figure, because he was known to be, you know, working with the Quds Force and he was known to be running a militia for the Iranians, and generally you didn't see him a whole lot. Recently, he has been very prominent. He has been puffing his chest out and making much of himself and making it clear that he is a strong fighter. That doesn't play well with the traditional, established Shia elites and, I think, with a lot of the Iraqi Shia population that is concerned about this.

So I think the dynamics are not positive for us, but they are complicated in ways that we could, I think, potentially be taking advantage of.

Ms. KELLY. Thank you.

I yield back.

Mr. POE. I thank the gentlelady.

The Chair will now recognize one of our newer members, as well, from the State of Illinois, Mr. Zeldin—New York. Sorry.

Mr. ZELDIN. That is okay. Thank you, Mr. Chairman.

And I appreciate everyone being here for this important hearing.

Taking a step back and, just generally, as we are watching the negotiations taking place between the Obama administration and the Iranian Government, I was struck, not too far back in history, when the State Department had indicated that they had reached a tentative deal, and the Iranian Government literally within 24 hours was refuting the terms of that agreement.

So who are we really negotiating—like, playing this out for a second, let's say over the course of the next month or so the President negotiates a deal just to negotiate a deal and it contains foolish concessions that can put the Iranian Government within 60, 90 days of being able to have a nuclear weapon. What is next?

From a 30,000-foot level, you are watching this unfold. And each of you have a lot of experience and background with this. What is next? What is the risk? Who are the players? What do we expect the Iranian Government to do next?

For me, personally, I don't trust them. I wish that, you know, instead of us reducing sanctions we would be increasing sanctions.

So just—I mean, it is an open question for you. But, you know, I have four experts here. I am able to ask this real basic question. Where are we going?

Mr. KAGAN. I think it is a great question, and I think it is a very important one.

You started to ask the question, who are we negotiating with? I actually think that is pretty clear. We are negotiating with the Supreme Leader. And there is a lot of, you know, rug-merchant negotiation going on, and the public statements don't necessarily shape me that much in terms of what the ultimate deal is going to look like, if there is going to be a deal. Everyone is shaping the environment.

But what is next? I think that if we have any kind of a deal that provides some kind of sanction relief—and I don't think we can have a deal the Iranians would accept that doesn't provide some kind of sanctions relief—I think Iranians will take advantage of that to try to stabilize their economy, to put through some economic reforms that they are working on, and to try to modernize their economy in a way that will make it more competitive and more self-sustaining.

There are some tensions in this regard, I think, between President Rouhani and Ayatollah Khomeini. Khomeini seems to want to drive for sort of autarky to make Iran completely independent from the international community so it will never be vulnerable to sanctions again. Rouhani is a better student of economics and seems to understand that that is not going to work.

But, for now, the dispute isn't very important, because they are clearly working on trying to get their economic feet underneath them, and any kind of sanctions relief in the first instance they will put toward trying to get that under control.

What will they then do? They will continue to pursue their objectives of driving us out of the region, establishing regional hegemony, and, of course, in my opinion, maintaining the ability to develop a nuclear weapon at the moment of their choosing.

Mr. BERMAN. Sir, if I could just add to what Dr. Kagan mentioned, I think the economic metrics are actually very compelling, and it is useful to sort of understand what we are looking at.

In 2012, as a result of U.S. and European sanctions levied on Iran, the Iranian economy constricted by roughly 5 percent. In 2013, it constricted by about 3 percent. Last year, it grew marginally as a result of sanctions relief, and it is on track this year to grow by between 1½ and 3 percent.

What this shows you is that, in the interim, in the year and a half that Iran has had greater breathing room, it has used that time judiciously to put its economic house in order. It has also, on a parallel track, as the State Department has noted, stepped up its sponsorship of global instability, as manifested in places like Syria and Yemen.

And so I think there is very much a causal relationship here. Terrorism is cheap, but it is not cost-free. The Iranian regime sees this as a deep-seated imperative. If it has more money, it is likely to invest more in it. I think it is quite as simple as that.

Mr. ZELDIN. Yeah.

You know, I see, obviously, the—we all see the economic benefit for Iran to be engaging in these negotiations. We see the strategic benefit for Iran. The problem is Iran is here and the U.S. here, Iran is here, the U.S. is here, Iran stays here, the U.S. is here.

And, you know, it is like here in American politics we are trying—you know, we have a President who is all politics all the time. His only version of compromise is to get it 100 percent his way. And now we are oversees with an enemy that does not respect weakness, they only respect strength.

I advocate for a stronger, more consistent foreign policy. We are negotiating with an element that is not our friend, who should not be trusted. They get these benefits, but they are going to be literally a turnkey away from, you know, having a nuclear weapon. They want to wipe Israel off the map. They will continue to be state sponsors of terrorism. The economic benefit will drive their efforts to be state sponsors of terrorism.

I am just—I am greatly concerned, and I do not trust that negotiating partner on the other side. And I appreciate the chairman for having this hearing to bring some light to it, because I hope that something cracks the code to turn the tide. That is why I welcome the Prime Minister coming here to address a joint session of Congress. And I hope that we don't make a deal just to make a deal.

I yield back.

Mr. POE. The gentleman yields back his time.

The Chair now will recognize the gentleman from California, Mr. Sherman, for his questions.

Mr. SHERMAN. I would point out that Reagan negotiated with Brezhnev, Roosevelt negotiated with Stalin. And so it is not a fair political attack to say Obama must be a bad President because he negotiates with Iran. You make peace, or try to make peace, with your enemies, not your friends. And, of course, we negotiated with North Vietnam as they were killing our troops on the ground.

Whatever deal is reached, or if a deal is reached, with the Iranians is basically a 2-year deal; that is to say, the President will use what he sees as his power to waive sanctions for 2 years.

I have come to listen to my Republican colleagues, and when asked what are the chances that their leader, Mr. Boehner, is going to bring to the floor the ''Thank God Obama is President and Did Such a Great Job of Negotiating a Superb Deal with Iran Act of 2015''—and I am asked what the chances of that are, I say, well, what are the chances that Julia Roberts calls me this afternoon?

So it is a 2-year deal, if there is a deal at all, subject then to the next Congress and the next President. It is guaranteed to be a poor deal because we are not in a position to get a great deal. What are our other options? The military option has barely been discussed here because it is highly unattractive, especially to the American people at this time.

And so I want to focus a little bit on sanctions. Iran doesn't just want a bomb. Nobody wants a bomb. You want half a dozen bombs. You certainly want to test one when you want to start being treated like a nuclear power.

And so we talk about sanctions. The most successful use of sanctions was against South Africa, which were universally embraced, totally multilateral, and took years to be effective.

So I would ask the panel here, help us draft the additional sanctions act, whether it is of 2015 or 2017—we might as well as start now; it is probably 2015.

But, also, comment on whether there are any sanctions you could imagine that wouldn't just threaten Iran with a mild recession, you know, negative-2-percent growth instead of positive-2-percent growth. Is there any sanction that you could suggest to us that would threaten the regime's survival in the timeframe it would take to create two or three nuclear weapons?

Dr. Byman?

Mr. BYMAN. As I am sure you know, Mr. Sherman, sanctions don't work quickly, right? If we look at South Africa as the shining example of their success, that was a decade-long process. And——

Mr. SHERMAN. And they didn't cause, like, rioting in the streets. They caused a decision by what ultimately was a government that made a rational decision. I mean, we deplore apartheid, but eventually that group—I mean, it was not the Supreme Leader that let Mandela out of jail and gave him the Presidency of the country.

Go on.

Mr. BYMAN. And the reason sanctions, I think, led Iran to the negotiating table was because they involved a wide array of U.S. Allies and Iranian trading partners and they hit Iran quite deeply. And to sustain sanctions and to make them more effective, you need that comprehensive approach. And we will only get that if our allies believe that we are not eager to reject a deal with Iran.

And so I don't think anyone trusts the Iranians. I have heard the President say repeatedly he does not trust the Iranians. But if we are seen as not negotiating, we will lose allied support, and that is bad for sanctions.

Mr. SHERMAN. I would point out that, unless we are willing to do the secondary sanctions approach—which is called for by present statute. But to say to Germany, ''You sell one paper clip to Iran, we are not going to let you send a single Mercedes to the United States,'' I mean, those are fighting words. That is outside the pale of our relationship with Europe. But unless we are willing to do that, Germany will sell nonlethal materials to Iran in a way that helps their economy just as soon as they are convinced that the United States is not behaving reasonably.

And, oh, by the way, if President Obama says we are not behaving reasonably, Congress will not be able to convince them to the contrary. Obama may not be popular with everybody in Congress; he is considerably more popular in Europe.

I will go on to the next witness, Mr. Badran. What is the Achilles' heel that we ought to be aiming at?

Mr. BADRAN. Well, I am no sanctions expert, but I think the oil sector, I think, was one of the areas that people were looking to to hit hard.

Mr. SHERMAN. Clearly, taking Kirk Menendez down to zero is, like, first on everybody's list of——

Mr. BADRAN. Right.

Mr. SHERMAN [continuing]. Additional sanctions.

Mr. Berman?

Mr. BERMAN. If you don't mind, I would like to amplify a point that you made about secondary sanctions on trading partners of the United States that also happen to be trading partners of Iran.

In this particular case, there is no country that looms larger than China. China consumes about 60 percent of Iranian total global oil exports, and it has ramped up consumption. Since the administration has applied a moratorium on reporting with regard to the 2010 Comprehensive Iran Sanctions, Accountability, and Divestment Act, the Chinese have actually increased their imports of Iranian oil, which means that, without Chinese acquiescence to trimming Iran's global economic footprint, it is going to be very difficult to really put Iran in a box in a meaningful way. And that means——

Mr. SHERMAN. So we can hurt their economy, but, without China, we can't threaten regime survival.

Mr. BERMAN. That is right.

Mr. SHERMAN. And so we would have to have not only the political gumption that it takes to be opposed to Iran, we would need to take on Walmart. I don't know if the people in the room are powerful enough to do that.

I will go on to Dr. Kagan.

Mr. KAGAN. Congressman, there is no magic silver bullet that we could, you know, pass along a sanction and take down the regime. And I wasn't aware that we were even talking about trying to take down the regime. The purpose of the sanctions——

Mr. SHERMAN. Well, in this room, many have said that this regime will hold on to its nuclear program unless it faces a risk to regime survival, that if it is just a matter of a bad day on the Tehran stock market or a bad year on the Tehran stock market, they would willingly pay that price.

Mr. KAGAN. I would need to think about whether I agree with that or disagree with it. But what I would say is that if the discussion is now about how to threaten the regime's survival, that is a very different context from the discussion in which we have been talking about sanctions hitherto, which have really been fundamentally focused on putting enough pressure on the regime to make the Supreme Leader change his calculus. And I agree with you that that is not going to be easy.

Mr. SHERMAN. I would just say nobody gives up their firstborn just to get a lower ATM fee.

And I yield back.

Mr. POE. I thank the gentleman.

Thank all members of the subcommittee for being here today, and especially our witnesses. It has been excellent.

All of your statements, official statements, will be made part of the record.

And this subcommittee is adjourned.

[Whereupon, at 4:15 p.m., the subcommittee was adjourned.]

APPENDIX

MATERIAL SUBMITTED FOR THE RECORD

SUBCOMMITTEE HEARING NOTICE
COMMITTEE ON FOREIGN AFFAIRS
U.S. HOUSE OF REPRESENTATIVES
WASHINGTON, DC 20515-6128

Subcommittee on Terrorism, Nonproliferation, and Trade
Ted Poe (R-TX), Chairman

TO: MEMBERS OF THE COMMITTEE ON FOREIGN AFFAIRS

You are respectfully requested to attend an OPEN hearing of the Committee on Foreign Affairs, to be held by the Subcommittee on Terrorism, Nonproliferation, and Trade in Room 2172 of the Rayburn House Office Building (and available live on the Committee website at http://www.ForeignAffairs.house.gov):

DATE: Wednesday, February 11, 2015

TIME: 2:00 p.m.

SUBJECT: State Sponsor of Terror: The Global Threat of Iran

WITNESSES: Frederick W. Kagan, Ph.D.
                   Christopher DeMuth Chair and Director
                   Critical Threats Project
                   American Enterprise Institute

                   Mr. Ilan I. Berman
                   Vice President
                   American Foreign Policy Council

                   Mr. Tony Badran
                   Research Fellow
                   Foundation for Defense of Democracies

                   Daniel L. Byman, Ph.D.
                   Professor
                   Security Studies Program
                   Edmund A. Walsh School of Foreign Service
                   Georgetown University

By Direction of the Chairman

COMMITTEE ON FOREIGN AFFAIRS

MINUTES OF SUBCOMMITTEE ON _____*Terrorism Nonproliferation and Trade*_____ HEARING

Day___*Wednesday*___Date___*February 11, 2015*___Room_____*2172*_____

Starting Time ____*2:00 p.m.*___Ending Time ___*4:15 p.m.*___

Recesses |___*1*___| (*2:47*to *3:26*) (____to_____) (____to_____) (____to_____) (____to_____) (____to_____)

Presiding Member(s)

Chairman Ted Poe

Check all of the following that apply:

Open Session ☑   Electronically Recorded (taped) ☑
Executive (closed) Session ☐   Stenographic Record ☑
Televised ☑

TITLE OF HEARING:

"State Sponsor of Terror: The Global Threat of Iran"

SUBCOMMITTEE MEMBERS PRESENT:

Reps. Poe, Issa, Perry, Zeldin, Keating, Sherman, Higgins, Kelly

---

NON-SUBCOMMITTEE MEMBERS PRESENT: *(Mark with an * if they are not members of full committee.)*

HEARING WITNESSES: Same as meeting notice attached? Yes ☑ No ☐
(If "no", please list below and include title, agency, department, or organization.)

STATEMENTS FOR THE RECORD: *(List any statements submitted for the record.)*

TIME SCHEDULED TO RECONVENE_____
or
TIME ADJOURNED ___*4:15 p.m.*___

Subcommittee Staff Director

www.ingramcontent.com/pod-product-compliance
Lightning Source LLC
Chambersburg PA
CBHW081145290526

45795CB00006B/2384